WHAT PEOPLE ARE SAYI.

DISCover the Power of You

This book leads you through a powerful journey of self-discovery, one that shows you the importance of self-awareness, how to create a culture where staff can perform at the highest level and more importantly a culture where staff feel rewarded, and empowered to make a difference.
Andrew Green, CEO Brighton Film School and Deputy Principal, Chichester College

They say that the only true and able helper is one that has suffered themselves. Someone who has found their own way out of the 'hole' – **disc**overing and using tools that work – who is then in a position to pass-it-on. Only when you have it can you start giving it away to others. This is precisely what Robert is doing – Take notice and believe, its powerful stuff!
Peter Mitchell, Yorkshire Coast Enterprise

If you are looking for something that makes sense of what has gone before and gives you a tool to make a real, long lasting cultural change within your organization, then you have found it here. This book is easy to read, sparks your own internal debates, makes you question what you thought you knew and drives you to try new things to see if they really do work. This book will give you the courage, the strength and the knowledge to break your own habits, challenge your beliefs and defaults and effectively stop you, your team, your organization from doing what you have always done, getting what you have always got, and start 'doing something different' and 'getting a whole lot better'.
Jayne Wilcock, Employment Education and Skills

An intriguing and stimulating alphabetical journey into the world of self-enlightenment. Robert Adams shines a light on the often complex areas of individual culture and leadership and writes in a deeply personal, highly accessible and yet self-deprecating style.

Duncan Lewis, Owner of Eaglei and contributor to the 'How's Business Guide to Starting a Business'

DISCover the Power of You

How to cultivate change for
positive and productive cultures

Robert Adams

DISCover the Power of You

How to cultivate change for positive and productive cultures

Robert Adams

BUSINESS BOOKS

Winchester, UK
Washington, USA

First published by Business Books, 2017
Business Books is an imprint of John Hunt Publishing Ltd., Laurel House, Station Approach,
Alresford, Hants, SO24 9JH, UK
office1@jhpbooks.net
www.johnhuntpublishing.com

For distributor details and how to order please visit the 'Ordering' section on our website.

Text copyright: Robert Adams 2016

ISBN: 978 1 78535 591 2
978 1 78535 592 9 (ebook)
Library of Congress Control Number: 2016954849

A CIP catalogue record for this book is available from the British Library.

Design: Stuart Davies

Printed and bound by CPI Group (UK) Ltd, Croydon, CR0 4YY, UK

We operate a distinctive and ethical publishing philosophy in all
areas of our business, from our global network of authors to
production and worldwide distribution.

CONTENTS

Acknowledgements

This book is dedicated to Justin, for his support and sufferance,
Mona, for her determined and decisive ways,
and my Mum, who will always be with me.

This book has been years in the brewing, if not in the writing, and my great spur has undoubtedly been Bev James, Millionaire Mentor and Author of DO IT! OR DITCH IT and The Coaching Academy who have inspired and challenged me to relook at my priorities, commitment and fundamental beliefs.

Many who know me in a professional setting will understand when I say that for years I wanted to be Helen Groves when I grew up. Helen is a renowned consultant in the education sector in the Yorkshire and Humber area. However, as the years progressed I came to realize I would probably never grow up and so Helen would have to be Helen and I would have to be me. It was only when I undertook my DISC training that I came to understand why this was, and could begin to revel in my impending ever-youthful old age. My thanks for this goes to Dave Pill, Master DISC Trainer.

The support and belief given, and example set, by my DISConnect colleagues has been invaluable, as have all the great dialogues that would otherwise go unrecognized by my never met friends, colleagues and connections on Facebook, LinkedIn and Twitter.

A very special thanks goes to Jayne Wilcock, Jane Gray, Andy Green, Peter Mitchell, Duncan Lewis and again Dave Pill who gave graciously of their time and expertise through reading and commenting on various parts of the book.

And a great thanks to John Hunt, Krystina Kellingley and Maria Barry of John Hunt Publishing Ltd for seeing the potential in my book.

Preface

It's a beautifully bright November morning. 11ᵗʰ of November 2015 to be precise. It's slightly crisp and chilly.

The smell of coffee permeates the room, with an undercurrent of treacle from the tarts, somehow in keeping with the ornate splendor of the wall paneling.

A hush descends and Bev James asks with a steely stare "What is your goal?"

I'm shaking slightly and worry that the others will notice.

But 'No' I'm saying to myself 'don't focus on that. I can do this' and so I start.

"I'm going to write a book…" but my mind is racing ahead of me. Do I sound pretentious, presumptuous, preposterous?

So instead of saying what I know I really want to say, my inner talk wins out.

I pull back.

I don't say 'within a year', but blurt out "…within the next five years."

A colleague stands; decisive, determined and direct "I'm also going to write a book, but I'm going to do it in a year."

I groan and spend the rest of the day kicking myself.

Writing a book has been a dream of mine for decades and is the culmination of years and years of questioning and searching for some resolution to the individual and cultural conundrum; the chicken and the egg, which comes first?

This book has gone through many permutations, from my B.A. (Hons) dissertation on 'alcohol misuse' as a consequence of what I perceived as my dysfunctional family. Sylvia Lafair, in her book *Unique*, said "all families are functional, and dysfunctional" – if only I had known that at the time. I worked my way through (very bad) comic book story lines, to penning a fantasy novel exploring the relationship between power and resistance, cultural identity and 'the flow' (a concept we now recognize to have strong connections to current thinking in the various fields of the neurosciences). That novel never got beyond the first draft before I was onto something new and even more exciting; a pattern I came to know intimately.

My MA in Diversity, Culture and Identity saw me delving into Identity Politics, with my research focusing greatly on personal, gendered, familial and national identity. Indeed, it was reflecting back on my roots that led to my second attempt at a novel. This was to be an historical fact-based novel tracking the lives of my family from my great grandparents on my Mum's side, and my step-family on the other side. Both my Granddad and my Step-Gran had fascinating stories to tell; from the Gorbals to India, Princesses to moon-shine; and from Ireland to the Gorbals, Politics to whisky galore. Stories that reflected only too well the destructive consequences of the demon drink and Colin Wilson's notion of energy loss through a lack of attention. Stories still to be told.

My 20 odd years as a practicing, exhibiting and professional artist with my key themes around intoxication, inebriation, identity and interconnectedness seemed somehow not to connect with my literary endeavors. And indeed the work that I did around my leadership and management MA and my years of experience in both management and leadership roles seemed also to sit outside this trajectory. Similarly, my years of teaching. I was a living example of DISConnectedness.

The lessons learnt from these various strands were filed away; successes highlighted on my CV; failures relegated to the dustbin of erased memories.

So here I am, seven years prior to my meeting with Bev James. I've been called into the Principal's office for a meeting with our HR Consultant (who's been brought in to sweep out the dead wood) and our Interim Principal, Little Ms. Timid As She Trod All Over You as she became known.

'So who's turn is it this time?' I'm thinking 'Which of my team will be no more?'

The College had gone into Notice to Improve just before I took up my senior management role. I'd taken my previous College through Action for Business Colleges Accreditation, being only the 6th College in the country to achieve this, and saw my current role as a stepping stone to Principalship; part of the senior team to bring the college back to good. It would look great on my CV. On taking up the post I made some immediate changes and measurable improvements. We were inspected within a few months of me starting and judged to be inadequate across the board, with my area one of the few showing 'green shoots.'

"Robert, we need to let you go." Little Ms. Timid As She Trod All Over You says. There is a silence I had never heard before in the room. All the learners who usually congregated outside in the courtyard seemed to have disappeared. The breeze that invariably fluttered the flipchart papers blue-tacked all around the walls from our strategic planning escapades lay flat and unflappable.

How could I not have known? Or even suspected?

"Do you want to say anything?"

What could I say? What was I supposed to say? I'd never been in this position before. Should I plead? Should I get angry and shout at her? Should I burst into tears?

I just nodded 'no' while channeling as much hatred into my stare as I could muster.

How fragile our minds can be! I had a long and successful track record and had secured Maxine Room OBE, then Principal/ Chief Executive of Park Lane College in Leeds, as my mentor. But as the saying goes 'you are only as good as your last performance.' I believed at the time, and for a long time after, that being made redundant was a major failing on my part. I put on a brave face.

But my confidence plummeted, my self-blame took hold and the sense of abandonment I thought I had long since dealt with came crashing back. I found I was unable to communicate what was going on with me to others, and I descended into a state of semi-depression. I felt alone, angry, guilty, totally confused and completely lethargic.

Anyway, I got another job, at a lower level, as a Quality Manager, and life carried on. We went through an Ofsted inspection and received a good with outstanding elements. But only too quickly things took a nose dive and this is where it really hit me about the impact our leaders have on the culture of our workplaces. Especially when there is too great a passivity, or worse collusion, from the rest of the management team that allows 'strategic drift' and 'toxic cocktail' to take hold. And in this respect I take full responsibility for my own unwillingness to confront the brewing situation. By now I had simply disengaged. We were inspected and judged to require improvement, and the proverbial shit hit the fan.

Over a three-year period, and one by one, my step-father, my dad, and my partner's dad died. Domino like. And then it happened…

I want to say right up front my Mum DID NOT die of liver failure.

"It's ironic," as more than one of my sisters noted.

My Mum's liver was in perfect working order. However, to say her death was not drink related would not be entirely true.

"I just thought I was just run down. You know, general hang-over symptoms," she said.

This led to a worsening respiratory issue and subsequent complications to her lungs.

"I know. I know. If I'd gone to the doctors when I was first ill, I'd have been treated by now. This time though, this time, definitely, when I get out of the hospital I 'really' will give up the drink this time."

This wasn't the first time my Mum had been in the hospital for drink related illnesses, but it was the last.

And I felt like I'd failed. At everything. As an artist, as a leader and manager, and most of all as a son; I hadn't saved her from my Dad; I hadn't saved her from my step-father; and I hadn't been able to save her from herself. My life just seemed to be rolling on, purposeless, unravelling to nowhere and my relationship was suffering. It was my partner who saw the advert for a two day Free Introduction to Coaching through The Coaching Academy and I went along in a rather skeptical manner. This led to the Diploma in Personal Professional Coaching, becoming a Licensed DISC Trainer, and a real bringing together of all my DISConnected strands that have so enriched my life.

When I first came upon DISC, which is the personality profiling framework I use throughout this book, I was blown away. It opened up an understanding of not just myself, my family and our dysfunctional past, of work cultures and the almost inevitability of the resulting successes and failures, but also of the whole gamut of interpersonal relationships we struggle with daily in our lives. It helped me understand my own and other people's identities and behaviors, and gave me the route map to a transformed future.

It's the 25th of February 2015, nine months prior to my November session with Bev James. It's damp, dreek and drizzly outside. I can see the droplets running down the window panes. The grey sky hangs there brooding.

The overhead strip lights try to compete giving the room a bright, too bright, unforgiving aspect.

There are in excess of 150 people in the room and Dave Pill, our trainer for the day, who I have already pegged as Mr. Bubbly, has just asked us to go to one end of the room or the other, depending on whether we think we are more outgoing and fast paced or more reserved and considered.

I'm momentarily uncertain, but then I remember Dave's instructions. It's not about how we are feeling right now, but about getting back to our basic wiring, our core selves, although within a designated environment, probably the work setting.

And I find myself, for the first time in a long time, vaguely smiling.

I kind of remember who I am. I remember my core self is outgoing and fast paced.

Dave then asks us to stay at the end of the room we have chosen, but to go to one side of the room or the other, depending on whether we think we are more task or more people orientated.

My social life is non-existent. I've withdrawn. I've lost my trust, my interest and my engagement. And yet again I smile, because I look over at Mr. Bubbly and really do remember who I am.

I am people orientated.

Dave now explains we are in the four quadrants of DISC. D.I.S.C.

I have a cheesy grin all over my face that I know will be fixed for some time to come. I AM an 'I'.

So it took me some time before realizing that all the strands in my circuitous route had simply been one journey amassing further questions, useful illustrations, experiences and knowledge in preparation for this book on the interplay between personality and culture; culture at the personal and the organizational level (whether the organization be business, family or friendships). And importantly I came to see how this knowledge can be used to counter the negativity I see at the heart of our culture that grates against the natural optimism of an 'I'. I came to see how my learning can be used to support myself and then others to cultivate the positive and productive cultures we all deserve.

Through the drafting of this book I have come to believe even more wholeheartedly than I had previously that the key drivers for me in doing this is twofold:

1 a making sense of my own personality, history, failings, dysfunctions and purpose,
2 and my growing irritation at many of the accepted 'facts' and 'truths' we live our lives by.

Later in the book I will question how culture relates to ideology and how ideology represents really no more than the prevailing interests of the dominant group in society (what became known as 'hegemony' from the writings of Antonio Gramsci who saw hegemony as a "moving equilibrium"). For me knocking this equilibrium off course is long overdue and is necessary for us all to start questioning our own personalities and approaches. Ultimately the learning that enabled me to strive to 'cultivate my own positive and productive culture' I believe will therefore be of benefit to others. And although the book is written primarily through the medium of organizational culture and leadership in particular the lessons learnt (which I add at the end of each section) are transferable to any and all walks of life.

As previously mentioned, during my time as a tutor, lecturer, manager, leader and consultant I have witnessed time and time again the impact leaders and changing leaders have had on the prevailing culture, and the impact cultures and changing cultures have had on individuals and teams; the positive and adverse effects on communication, conflict, performance, business success and individual wellbeing. I am convinced culture and success do not happen by accident. Cultural drift however does happen through inattentiveness.

The culture you cultivate or neglect will either help or hinder your bottom-line.

More immediately this book came out of a melting pot set in motion through two articles I wrote and posted on Facebook, Twitter and LinkedIn; the first entitles 'Whose personality is it anyway?' and its follow up 'Whose culture is it anyway?' After these initial articles it was all but impossible not to carry on and elaborate my thinking.

I have written this book therefore on the one hand for individuals who have a desire to better understand their own personality, people who may be aspiring to become great leaders in whichever field or area they are in and at whichever level in a business or organization they are at. And more specifically, I have written this book for anyone looking to raise their own self-awareness, confidence and understanding to cultivate positive changes to the cultures they find themselves or place themselves in. I have written this book for;

- People who have lost their confidence or lost their way.
- People who have become stuck in thinking or behavioural patterns that no longer suit, or a role, a career, a life they no longer resonate with.
- People who have lost touch with their core self, core values and so their core purpose.

I have been driven to do this because I passionately believe it is my responsibility and your responsibility as leaders, aspiring leaders and individuals to transform ourselves, to transform the world we live in for the better. This is sorely needed as we shift into a new phase of 'being.' Bookshelves are awash with literature of an imminent transformation of Homo Sapiens; how we live, how we think, how we do business, and how we organize ourselves. Are we really shifting to a networked culture? Is the end of capitalism really upon us?

My belief is that if we want to survive and indeed thrive in our new world, whatever that looks like, we will need high levels of

self-awareness and cultural literacy, that is, individual personality, organizational personality and networked personalities. To
use the oft quoted Mahatma Ghandi, "you need to be the change
you wish to see in the world" and as the great Gestaltist Fredrick
Perls noted "change occurs when one becomes what he is, not
when he tries to become what he is not."

**The purpose of this book is to transform people, to
transform the world we live in.**

This is all very lofty but what does it mean practically in a
business context? You will need to understand:

- what drives and motivates your own thinking and
  behaviour;
- what drives and motivates your staff, customers, stakeholders (and family, friends and neighbours) – the dreaded
  'other';
- what constitutes effective communications for reduced
  internal conflict and increased customer satisfaction;
- what defines success and how to better re-define success
  to shift from a preoccupation with money, sales and
  profits; from what I can get out of the business or the
  business can get out of its customers, to what I can 'give'
  to ensure success for our people (customers, staff, and
  ourselves through finding what Colin Wilson calls our
  'inner freedom'), our planet (larger community and
  indeed global concerns), for our businesses (and our
  profits), and for progress (sustainability for future generations), what is often referred to as the quadruple bottom-
  line.

This will require a shift from an ego driven approach to a
distributed and networked attitude, through a growth win-win

mentality. For all of this to happen there will need to be a willingness to truly engage in the life long journey of learning and self-awareness to understand our own 'why?'; our own purpose. This will necessitate a turning away from the negativity that pervades much of our current cultural norms and embracing a true 'yes' to life. A yes to life that means we are willing to confront and challenge some of our own long held beliefs and unconscious values to really relook at and renew our sense of purpose.

This book is by no means the end of my search, nor has it answered all my questions. What it is, is a learning journal on my highly circuitous and interesting journey. My hope therefore is that this book will offer you some support on your own learning journey. The kind of support, and all in one place, I would have greatly appreciated and benefited from had I had access to it back in the day.

Part One

Introduction

To better understand (let alone positively cultivate) the cultures we find ourselves in; in life in general, in our organizations and in our businesses, we need a far better understanding of people. Ourselves first and foremost. Then our colleagues, our staff, our customers, our competitors, our partners, our families and friends, our neighbors; all those dreaded 'others.'

- What motivates people to do what they do?
- What motivates people to buy what they buy?
- What do our staff and customers, family and friends, really want?
- How can we best communicate with them?
- What mechanisms and styles are best suited to communicating with them, and communicating the message we want to convey?
- How might we alienate our staff or customers, family and friends?
- How might we win them over?
- What desires, needs and fears do we and others bring to any interrelationship or business transaction?
- And, that BIG question, who am I?

These and many other questions are perennial in life in general, as well as in the business world. As individuals and business leaders in an ever changing world, we need to find ways to access this information efficiently and effectively. This is where DISC personality profiling comes in. DISC is the longest running and most widely researched profiling framework in the world. DISC is derived from Dr. William Marston's behavioral model in the late 1920s and has been further developed since that time. Nevertheless, DISC is the simplest and easiest to use personality profiling framework for 'normal' behavior around. DISC is the personality framework I will expand on and explain further in this introductory section. DISC will underlie all our subsequent discussions throughout this book in relation to people and culture, and act as a way in to my A to Z Framework and its associated sub-models.

First though let me remind you of my starting point; my initial article entitled 'Whose Personality is it Anyway?' which I wrote as a means to try and clarify in my own mind how DISC personality profiling related to coaching;

Whose Personality is it anyway?

You might have heard the one about the Buddhist retort 'whose religion is it anyway?' when confronted by western critics, and then you might have wondered,

- 'What is this really all about?',
- or 'Who's who?',
- or 'Why are we questioning this?',
- or possibly 'How will we find out?'

Whichever question this raises for you will have indicated a preferred, or 'default', way of looking at things.

If you know your own and other's 'default' traits you will be in a position to communicate more effectively, cut off potential conflict situations at the pass, and influence your own or your team's potential for success. This is at the heart of personality profiling; with DISC being the longest running most widely used, and most comprehensively researched model.

DISC offers a means to understand yourself and others in a matter of minutes and is therefore an invaluable coaching tool. DISC stands for Dominant, Influencer, Steady and Conscientious. These are the four main personality traits which correspond to;

- Dominant - 'outgoing, task orientated',
- Influencer - 'outgoing, people orientated',
- Steady - 'reserved, people orientated',
- Conscientious - 'reserved, task orientated'.

So how can this help in coaching sessions?

First, by identifying their own traits Coaches will be able to guard against their own biases, ways of seeing things and imposing their perceptions onto you, the client. And secondly, by identifying their client's main traits they will be able to better adapt their coaching style to suit their client's needs. Examples of this might be;

- for a D client Coaches will want to keep the pace brisk, while for an S client Coaches will want to ensure a steady pace,
- for an I client Coaches might need to support their client to refocus, while for a C client Coaches might need to support them to see the big picture and not get bogged down in the detail,
- for a D client Coaches might need to challenge how realistic the goal is in the timeframe, while for an S client Coaches might need to challenge them to step out of their comfort zone,
- for an I client Coaches might want to check out their overly optimistic assessment of reality, while for a C client Coaches might want to confirm just how perfect perfect needs to be.

So how can you easily identify which main traits a client has (in mere minutes)?

Like coaching itself a Coach might take a GOAL orientated approach;

1 Get their client to pick which of the four key words best describes them; Dominant, Influencer, Steady, Conscientious.

2 Observe their clients behavior and approach. Are they direct? Are they interactive? Are they steady or shy? Are they considered and questioning?

3 Ask their client if they think they are more outgoing or reserved, more task or people orientated.

4 Listen to the language their client uses. Are they interested in 'what?' and the bottom-line? Are they interested in 'who?' and people? Are they interested in 'why?', security or harmony? Are they interested in 'how?' and getting things right?

Paying attention to what motivates others will ensure Coaches give their clients what they need to progress, develop and succeed. While paying attention to their own personality traits and motivations will ensure a more heightened self-awareness that will ultimately support the success of their own coaching practices and business.

My subsequent article 'Whose culture is it anyway?' was to be more nebulous and while relating to organizational culture left me highly dissatisfied about any clarity on what culture really was, what impact if any it had on the business, how it could be managed, and how it related to individual people. So let me remind you:

Whose culture is it anyway?

You might have read my article 'whose personality is it anyway?' which was all about the individual, but how does this relate to your business or organization on a more macro level?

Dr. William Marston identified four main personality traits which correspond to 'outgoing, task orientated', 'outgoing, people orientated', 'reserved, people orientated' and 'reserved, task orientated'; usually shown as a circle of four quadrants, with each trait bleeding into the next. These became known as the four main personality traits - DISC: Dominant, Influencer, Steadiness and Conscientious.

Yuval Noah Harari in his book *Sapiens: A Brief History of Humankind* stated, "The immense diversity of imagined realities that Sapiens invented, and the resulting diversity of behavior patterns, are the main components of what we call 'culture'," which allowed us (Sapiens) to create "the mythical glue that binds together large numbers of individuals..."

Culture then is a form of myth making and imaginative story-telling that speaks to the inter-subjective aspect of our consciousness, transmitted through 'memes', i.e. a unit of cultural transmission (what the post-structuralists call discourse). Memes will transmit the reason an organization, nation, global conglomerate exists and the culture it conveys; that is, the organization or nation or global personality.

So, to come back to our question 'whose culture is it anyway?' we first need to ask 'which culture?';

- our individual culture (personality),
- our local collective culture (which might be our family or our business),
- our national culture (our nation),
- or our global culture (the planet)?

For any of these cultures will contain remnants of the others, with some having a key and direct impact on what and how we do things.

When considering our own businesses, the culture is likely to be set through a combination of our own 'default' personality traits, our leadership style, our staff's personality traits, our followers behavior, and the inter-relationship between these various aspects. There is a well knows saying 'always a leader, never a follower be' which sorely misunderstands the relationship between leader/follower and the role followers play in enabling or crippling success.

In the West we are highly driven by leadership cultures that have come out of the command and control approach. However, with the rise in social networks and a belief in empowerment and egalitarianism this approach is no longer appropriate or effective. And indeed is counter to the needs of our 'complex dynamic system' with high levels of uncertainty and ambiguity. In our current and future business world real control for leaders and followers alike will come through self-awareness and self-management.

Our future culture/s need to be shared ones, based on motivational factors of trust and respect, underlined by congruent value and belief systems. This is counter to our existing dominant approach, but is a trajectory everyone who believes they deserve input into 'owning' their culture can influence.

Self-awareness

So what does this have to do with me, my failures and successes, and my learning? As we progress through the A to Z sections one of the key themes we will touch on is the need for high levels of self-awareness, a commodity decidedly lacking in my earlier life. Self-awareness we now know is the root of emotional intelligence. We also know that emotional intelligence has more impact on success than IQ (traditional knowledge based intelligence). It was this lack of self-awareness in myself and in those around me that led to many of the resulting conflicts, dysfunction and what I came to understand later as internal dissonance. A dissonance brought about by a lack of alignment between my lived behavior, my professed ideals, the beliefs of those around me and the dawning realization that my so called intellect was not really getting me anywhere I really wanted to go. This general heady mix and the accompanying sense of confusion only seemed to lead to more conflict and frustration, and general lethargy in which to counter this situation.

The slow dawning of my self-awareness through self-reflection and reflection on others and my various situations and encounters fueled what subsequently became my passion for learning about the self, self-culture and other-culture. This in turn has led to my growing belief that while we talk a lot about self-awareness this is driven through a larger socialization prism that effectively limits our ability to self- or other-reflect beyond given parameters. It is this prison we need to break free from. And it is this that has fueled my A to Z Framework and MIRROR Model in particular.

Self-awareness is underscored by a number of core concepts that we have alluded to above. We first need to get to grips with these before getting into the nitty gritty of the book. These concepts are values, beliefs, purpose and of course culture itself. We will also need clarity around what we mean by leadership and how leadership styles impact on other people, cultures and so your bottom-line in life or in business. And most importantly a continued elaboration and depth of understanding around personality, primarily our own as the vehicle to understand ourselves and others, our interactions and engagements within different settings and environments, and how our own personality sets our own culture.

Few organizations I've worked in, or worked with, have focused overly much on cultures directly or explicitly. Values will be set and put on a lovely plaque. Strategies will be written and distributed through high quality brochures. And in some organizations and businesses standards, expectations and codes of conduct will be polished off in HR, passed down through line management and on occasion may even be mentioned in performance reviews.

One such organization I worked with had its values, mission and strategic objectives proudly displayed in hallways, offices, online and as headers on employee review documentation. Leaders, and even managers, would 'tell' staff about their values of inclusion, 'inform' them of their mission to be consultative, and 'berate' them about the need for respect. Performance plummeted and objectives went unmet.

The senior team called in the consultants and were dismayed at their findings that there was a mismatch between stated values and actual practices. How could that have happened? Who was to blame? And so the big ship slowly, ever so slowly, began to turn.

Values, beliefs, purpose, leadership and culture

Values are the abstract concepts that drive the choices we make. There is a huge body of research in the academic and business worlds which shows that values have a major influence on how we act, behave and perform, and so it really is imperative that as individuals and leaders we set our core values and the core values of our businesses explicitly. Yet how many of us actually do this? The Business Directory states that values are *"Important and lasting beliefs or ideals shared by the members of a culture about what is good or bad and desirable or undesirable."* What it could have stated more explicitly is that these shared values are mostly unconscious and rarely investigated let alone reflected on.

The Coaching Academy defines values as *"The moral principal or accepted standards of a person or group."* When we think that our values are mostly unconscious this is really quite frightening. The importance of this is raised even further once we realize there are actually two different set of values, what are called 'idealistic' values and 'operational' values.

Idealistic values are those values we really want to have, but don't necessarily act out or behave regularly (if ever). Operational values are the values we display daily through our actions (mostly unconsciously). This chimes well with what are often referred to as our 'core' values and our 'practices'; related to the analogy of the 'onion' that Hofstede, Hofstede and Minkov talk about in *Cultures and Organizations* where our core values are fairly static around pairings; good or bad, normal or abnormal. The problem arises when we do not routinely interrogate what is accepted as good or bad, normal or abnormal while living in a world that is changing round about us at an ever increasing pace. So we end up living by a set of outmoded values which are no longer fit for purpose.

If we return to Hofstede's 'onion' analogy where the outer rings of the onion (the visible elements) change at a faster pace than the inner ring (our core and unconscious values) we can see how this layering affects our daily lives.

1 The first and fastest paced changing ring of the onion is called our 'symbols'. We only have to think about the world of fashion, or the changing nature of language through texting.

2 With the second ring being our 'heroes' and prized characters. You only need to consider the rise of celeb culture.

3 And the third and slower changing ring of the onion being our 'rituals' and social activities. Consider the dwindling numbers engaged in religious practices in the UK.

Some common values, to take a random selection of 10, might be;

- Authenticity
- Compassion
- Creativity
- Fairness
- Honesty
- Kindness
- Learning

- Respect
- Spirituality
- Wisdom

Self-reflection

- You might want to take some time to consider and list your own top 10 values.

We would need to look at our day to day actions and behavior to determine our operational values (we will look at this aspect later in the book, see section C). The key is to be able to set goals and future plans that can incorporate both our idealistic and operational values.

Values are highly important in a business context as they sum up what your business stands for; what makes you special. They educate and clarify for your clients and potential customers what the 'identity' of the business is. Having a clear set of values that speak to the public then offers a highly competitive advantage. Also, values help businesses in their decision-making processes. For example, if one of your core values is 'quality' then any product or service that does not reach a satisfactory standard are improved, replaced or eliminated. Every business is different and will have its own core values - whether consciously articulated or unconsciously enacted.

The trick is to align our idealistic and operational values.

Some common business values, again taking a selection of 10, might be;

- Innovation
- Creativity
- Diversity

- Excellence
- Fairness
- Growth
- Community partnership
- Respect
- Sustainability
- Win-win

Self-reflection

- Why don't you take a few moments to consider and list a few core values your business currently holds?
- And take a few minutes to consider the values you wish to cultivate if different to those your business or organization already holds?

A point to bear in mind is that due to values being abstract concepts (usually single words) their meaning can be very different from one person to another. So when setting these for your business never assume the whole team attach the same meaning to the words set. Value setting in an organizational or business context needs to be done as a group activity.

It is interesting to note that as part of the direct research I carried out towards writing this book many of the above business values were highlighted. But worryingly there were just as many respondents, both leaders and managers, who lacked clarity around their company or organizations values; some respondents confused their mission for their values, while others stated they didn't know if the organization had set any values at all.

So what, you might ask, is driving them?

Beliefs
Beliefs are the things we hold to be true, but which we require no

evidence for. They are the things which allow us or stop us from doing things. Beliefs are passed on to us through our various cultural settings; our parents and family, teachers, friends and peers, the media and the different groups we belong to. Beliefs are set as part of the socialization process in early childhood and adolescence. The Business Directory defines beliefs as; *"Assumptions and convictions that are held to be true, by an individual or a group, regarding concepts, events, people, and things."*

An understanding therefore of your own and your team's beliefs are important for your life and business as these will determine what you, your team and the business can and can't do, who can and can't be liked or worked with, how things can and can't be done, and why things should or shouldn't be done.

Beliefs therefore are extremely powerful things that support or hinder your personal success, or the success of your business.

We know there is currently a great deal of research being undertaken in the field of neuroscience around how the brain works, emotions and how these affect our decision-making processes and abilities (see my recommended reading list at the end of this book for useful references). The good news is that the findings from this research clearly show that beliefs and so habits of thought and behavior can be changed as well as reinforced. Old beliefs set in childhood can be modified or completely reprogrammed to better suit your current situation and needs. This is by no means an easy process but we now know the steps required and therefore have no 'excuses' for not addressing our limiting beliefs.

So, what exactly do I mean by limiting beliefs?

Limiting beliefs are those things that are no longer good for you to believe, the thoughts that are holding you back. Have you ever heard yourself or others say things like?

"I can't..."

"I don't..."

"We don't do that here."

"It's not the done thing."

"I'm not..."

"I should..."

"I shouldn't..."

When you hear any of these you are hearing examples of limiting beliefs. When you hear these in yourself or your business they are the things it is imperative you question.

Limiting beliefs stop you or your business achieving more than you or your business currently are.

Your mindset determines what actions you take in your business. Your limiting beliefs, by definition, limit your decision-making potential and so the actions open to you. It is imperative you eliminate as many of your, or your teams, limiting beliefs as possible. Someone once said, 'all great experts are learners first.' Remember you are the expert in your life and your business.

Self-reflection

Can you think of any limiting beliefs within your organization that is holding the business back? List any you have heard here;

I/we don't...

I/we should...

I/we shouldn't...

I/we must...

I/we mustn't...

I/we can't...

I/we can't...

I/we can't...

At their extreme limiting beliefs can be actively disastrous for you or your business.

It is worrying, again from the research I carried out directly towards writing this book, that so many leaders and managers were unable to articulate limiting beliefs; their own, their teams or their organizations. Respondents tended to focus on rigidity of systems and procedures or issues of funding and finance which they viewed as 'real' practical limitations to growth. They were mostly ill prepared to discuss inner psychological or cultural limiting beliefs.

This is fascinating as we will see as we progress through this book's journey, as it illustrates well our over-reliance on logic when we know what drives us is first and foremost our instincts and then our emotions. Logic is merely how we explain away our instinctive and emotionally driven behaviors.

Purpose

There are few people who would honestly admit to being fulfilled and finding their 'purpose' in our routine nine to five lives. Indeed, few people would be able to articulate what their purpose in life is. It took Viktor E Frankl four years in the concentration camps to learn what Nietzsche had already pointed out "He who has a *why* to live can bear with almost any *how*." If we have a purpose, we can thrive rather than survive. This is scary stuff. For Viktor E Frankl it is how we use our values when placed in difficult and scary circumstances that will dictate whether or not we are worthy of our purpose. However, identifying and then living by your values and purpose can be a very difficult, tumultuous, lonely and frightening road.

Is it so surprising most people take the road of least resistance?

In the business world we are used to hearing about vision, mission and principles. A vision is what the business wants to achieve at some point in the future. This is aspirational and inspirational to motivate and focus your staff, customers and partners. The mission is what the business currently does, how it does it and who it does it for. Your mission helps you in your day to day decision-making. Principles are the ethical and agreed ways of doing business, often related to regulatory requirements. However, what is too often missing is the purpose of the business; the 'why?' Is it surprising then that so few people find fulfillment in your business or in their work?

My own findings correlate to this, with most leaders, managers and business owners I have spoken to about the purpose of their business offering up 'what they do' or 'how they do it', with very few enthusing about the 'why.'

Simon Sinek offers a great overview of this with his 'Golden Circle' concept, related to new developments in our understanding of how the brain works. As Sinek explains it, there is an outer circle, the neocortex, which is the 'what?' - what your business does. There is then an inner circle, the limbic, which has two levels. The outer level is the 'how?' - how your business will do what it says it will. This is often considered to be the unique selling point (USP) of your business. Sinek though has shown through his work that it is the lower level of the limbic brain that really sells your business. The 'why?' - why your business does what it does. This is the core purpose of your businesses existence. Indeed, we now know from research carried out on the brain in relation to story-telling that it is our biology that drives our emotions, such as the release of oxytocin (the feel good chemical) when we hear good aspects in a story, or the release of dopamine from our limbic (reward center) that triggers feelings of hope and optimism when we hear happy endings. As Sinek says, *"People don't buy what you do. People buy why you do it."* This is equally true for individuals as it is for businesses. Ask yourself, what is your purpose?

Antony Jenkins, CEO of Barclays, is quoted as saying,

> *"Purpose is not an add-on, it's not an initiative. It is a culture change and it never finishes."*

Sir Richard Branson, best known as founder of the Virgin Groups, asks,

> *"How are you bringing Purpose to your business or job?"*

Self-reflection
Why not take some time to consider;

- your own purpose (your why),
- and the purpose (the why) of your business.

Scientific research shows a clear correlation between people with purpose in their lives and the fact they tend to be less prone to disease. Psychologists align purpose to wellbeing. And many business experts are now waking up to the fact that purpose is the key to improved performance and great success. Purpose therefore is more and more becoming seen as the route map through complexity and ambiguity (we will discuss these terms further in section B), with leaders seen as the navigators. Finding your leadership purpose then will not only support your own wellbeing, but the wellbeing of your business or organization.

Leadership
Many people reading this book might be aware that the first real theories around leadership came from Nicolo Machiavelli in his

book *The Ruler*. Machiavelli's portrayal of leadership is one of manipulation, deceit and murder; less a theory and more an observation of practices at the time. Since Machiavelli's days there have been many different takes on leadership, but what do we actually mean when we say we are leaders?

The Eight Dimensions of Leadership states "To be a leader is to make tough decisions – often being forced to choose between competing demands – but what makes it a truly messy endeavor is the fact that people are involved." In the book *Neuroscience for Leadership* they define leaders as those who *"have sufficient status, power, dominance and influence in a group to be able to achieve innovatory goals with and through others."* Which matches quite closely to the Online Business Dictionary which states that leaders are those *"that holds a dominant or superior position within its field, and is able to exercise a high degree of control or influence over others."*

Leadership then is seen to be held by those in a position of power who make effective decisions and take effective action to achieve things through effective interactions with other people. As Charles Handy said in his seminal book *Understanding Organizations, "… call it chairman or coordinator, representative or organizer, there is a need in all organizations for individual link-pins who will bind groups together…"*

Travis Bradberry, author of *Emotional Intelligence 2* and *The Personality Code*, defines leadership as *"a process of social influence which maximizes the efforts of others toward the achievement of a greater good."* For Bradberry the key in this respect is *social influence*, not authority or power. This definition really takes leadership out of a narrow concern with organizational decision-making and places it into the wider domain of all walks of life and all interrelationships aimed at cultivating positive and productive cultures.

Bradberry's definition also raises questions around what we mean by the notion of power and authority. If we turn to the field of philosophy, we can see how your very 'personality' shapes your philosophy and so why it has been all but impossible to gain one coherent picture about the truth of power.

- Hobbes, for instance, believed power to be concentrated in the hands of the few and exerted by external coercion and force. In DISC parlance, which we will expand on in the next section, this is very much a 'C' stance where the environment is unfavorable and you lack the power or control needed to change it.

- Nietzsche's 'will to power' expands this conflict view of power, advocating though that all individuals crave power over others, conveying a 'D' stance where the environment is unfavourable but you do have, or are able to take, power or control.

- On the other-hand the pluralist theorist Dahl believed power to be dispersed among the many or based on a consensus. This is very much an 'S' stance where the environment is more favourable, although you lack the individual power or control needed to change it.

- While the post-structuralist Foucault believed that power is productive, that is, that it is exercised rather than possessed, so circulating throughout the social body rather than emanating from the top down. An 'I' stance where the environment is favourable and you are able to exercise some level of power and control.

We can see then from the above, admittedly very limited overview, the impact our personalities have on our thinking. This is most clearly seen in our 'default' approaches to our own leadership styles.

This reflects well to the styles and approaches I have seen throughout my years in management and leadership, where leadership and management styles very clearly correlate to individual personality traits, such as;

- ***D's*** *who describe their leadership style as determined, solutions focused, choosing the right tool at the right time.*
- ***I's*** *who describe their leadership style as open, positive, enthusiastic, outgoing and influencing.*
- ***S's*** *who describe their leadership style as maternalistic, protective, democratic, decisions through discussion.*
- ***C's*** *who describe their leadership style as task driven, involving people to make sure tasks are done.*

I will elaborate on DISC later in the Introduction and refer to it thereafter throughout this book.

There have been lots written about the connection between leadership and culture and the impact they have on one another, both positive and negative. In fact, too much for this book to be about that in itself, or it would just be another one of the many. This book has a more specific remit which is to look at cultural cultivation in relation to personality and offer a clear route map from our 'default' positions.

Culture

So what do we mean when we talk about culture? First, the online Oxford Dictionary defines culture as;

1 the arts and other manifestations of human intellectual achievement regarded collectively.
2 the ideas, customs, and social behavior of a particular people or society.

Some other online definitions are:

- the cumulative deposit of knowledge, experience, beliefs, values, attitudes, meanings...
- the systems of knowledge shared by a relatively large group of people.

There is a passage I love in Yuval Noah Harari's book *Sapiens: A Brief History of Humankind* that highlights explicitly an element that underlies the definitions above; that being the 'invented reality' of culture.

"The immense diversity of imagined realities that Sapiens invented, and the resulting diversity of behavior patterns, are the main components of what we call 'culture'."

Culture for Harari starts about 70,000 years ago with the Cognitive Revolution which is the point at which Homo Sapiens learned the ability to transmit three different kinds of things:

1 information about the world,
2 information about social relations,
3 and information about things that do not really exist.

This allowed Sapiens to create *"the mythical glue that binds together large numbers of individuals..."*

Culture then is a nebulous term, a form of myth making and imaginative story-telling that speaks to, what Harari calls, the inter-subjective aspect of our consciousness, transmitted through 'memes.' Memes is the cultural equivalent to our organic transmission through 'genes.' The best known description of this is by Dr. Martin Farncombe in a series of articles about practical memetics.

Briefly, memes are 'a unit of cultural transmission' that we share through language, characteristics, social customs, beliefs, systems etc, etc (remember, what the post-structuralists call discourse). In organizational context memes will transmit the reason an organization exists and the culture it conveys. However, as this is a construct there is no inherent truth to it other than the fact the majority believe it to be so. Culture then is an ambiguous concept, which frames (in an imperfect way) the prevailing ideology or interests of the dominant group. It maps what is 'in' and what is 'out'. It therefore leads to subcultures that need to be controlled or contained, or better still 'naturalized'; what theorists term assimilated into the prevailing hegemony. As not everyone will absorb memes to the same degree there will at times be conflict between the dominant culture and sub-cultures, and between individual and organizational beliefs. This is why some people 'fit' and others don't (we will expand on cultures further in section C).

So cultures, it seems, need to be encompassing enough to allow an individual to fit or 'choose' to buy into the prevailing cultural norms, or if they cannot fit can at least be 'controlled or contained' within them. It is this assimilationist approach that I believe is one of the key factors that is inhibiting real progress in society and does nothing to challenge the assumption that we must live by the hegemonic views of the dominant group. So long as this assumption is allowed to go unchallenged we will never be able to move beyond our limited cultural beliefs and our restricted comfort zones.

It is the element of 'choice' mentioned above that was identifiably missing through the research I gathered around cultural questioning in preparation for this book. Respondents gave a very mixed picture with lots of confusion; some seeing Objectives as the Culture, some offering a recognition of 'denial' at leadership level, most seeing the culture as the sole responsibility of the most senior leader, and very few seeing other individuals, the team or the customers as having any input into shaping the culture. Due to this, a positive culture, it was felt, is dependent on good communication and leadership from the very top one or few, or things can quickly become 'toxic.'

What we need to keep in mind is that while there is culture at the organizational, national and international levels there is also culture at the individual level; what we call personalities and sub-personalities. We shall discuss the notion of sub-personalities in section T.

DISC personality profiling

So what is this DISC (personality profiling) that keeps rearing it head and has already been referred to quite a bit? As Gareth Morgan put it in *Images of Organization*,

There is no truth, only personality.

Let's take an historical tour first. The 'rule of four' has been around for centuries. The first recorded reference to these being Empedocles' four elements Earth, Air, Fire and Water which he related (in homage) to the mythical gods that ruled the world 444 years B.C. Ancient Greece saw an explosion in population, commerce, technology and intellect that still influences our thinking to this day. Hippocrates, the great Greek physician, developed his thinking around the 'humors', the body fluids that caused our moods, emotions and behaviors. These body fluids were called;

- yellow bile which related to active types,
- blood which related to lively types,
- phlegm which related to slow types,
- black bile which related to dark types.

As the work in the fields of medicine advanced these 'humors' where updated to 'temperaments' and a more nuanced understanding of personality developed, becoming;

- choleric which related to active, ambitious and assertive types,
- sanguine which related to lively, impulsive and sociable types,
- phlegmatic which related to slow, stable and supportive types,
- melancholic which related to thoughtful worriers and cautious types.

It wasn't until the early 20th century, almost two thousand years later, that these 'temperaments' were reconsidered through the developing fields of psychology and psychiatry. Carl Gustav Jung, the renowned Swiss psychologist, published his theories on 'psychological types' which he defined as;

- thinking,
- feeling,
- sensation,
- intuition,

which he further sub-dividing into introverts and extroverts.

However, the work in the fields of medicine, and the new fields of psychology and psychiatry, were based on trying to gain a better understanding of illness and deviance. Dr. William Marston took a different tack and decided he wanted to investigate normal people rather than ill or abnormal people. He published his work, *The Emotions of Normal People*, in 1928. It was here Dr. Marston elaborated on his DISC theory. For Marston there were two axes; the horizontal and the vertical. Again our 'rule of four.'

The key, for Dr. Marston, was our perception and interaction with the environment we find ourselves in (remember our discussion on power).

The key questions to be posed were:

- Is this a favourable or unfavourable environment?
- Do I have the power to change or control this environment?

Your responses to your environment will determine in which of the four quadrants you sit:

- A person who thinks the environment is **not** favourable, but believes they **can** change or control it will exhibit a Dominant style.
- A person who thinks the environment **is** favourable, and believes they **can** change or control it will exhibit an Influencer style.
- A person who thinks the environment **is** favourable, but believes they have **no** control over it will exhibit a Steady and supportive style.
- A person who thinks the environment is **not** favourable, and believes they have **no** control over it will exhibit a Conscientious style.

This is the foundations of DISC: Dominant, Influencer, Steadiness, Conscientious.

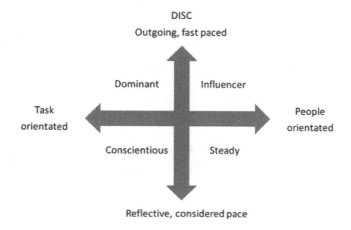

Before moving on to an overview of each of the four personality styles it is important to recognize that DISC is not about labelling people. DISC is about recognizing we all have *predictable* ways of behaving in particular situations. But we can practice the use of other personality styles to support us in different environments through raising our self-awareness.

We are each a 'blend' of personality styles, usually having one dominant and one secondary style (although not always) but it is important to understand each of the individual styles first to get real depth of knowledge around each of the personality styles motivations, approaches, strengths, weaknesses and fears. This way we can really begin to see what each style (and so blends of styles) can bring to different situations, to the organization or business, and what this might mean for our leadership and communication styles to really cultivate the culture if we want ourselves individually and collectively, and our businesses holistically, to thrive in today and tomorrows changing environment.

D – Dominant

- Anyone of a certain age reading this might have heard the Frank Sinatra song 'I did it my way.' That could very well be the D mantra. People who have a D style are outgoing and task orientated. These styles tend to be Decisive, Determined, Driven and Driving, Doers and of course Dominant. They will be motivated by being in control or having a challenge. Their approach will be fast paced and direct.

- D's have real strengths around seeing the big picture, goal setting, finding solutions, being focused on the bottom-line and so ensuring the productivity of themselves and those they work with. D's nevertheless can have a number of key weaknesses, such as, being overly blunt, aggressive and overly Demanding and Domineering in their drive to succeed, coming from their fear of failure. Remember Ivana Trump's quip 'Don't get even. Get everything', coming out of Vince Lombardi's famous quote 'Winning isn't everything…it's the only thing!' This drive to win can be sorely undermined by their weaknesses noted above as well as not analysing the detail closely enough and being too quick to act.

• As a leader D's tend to be forceful and strong willed, they like power and authority and are likely to communicate through 'telling' others what to do. They are likely to decide what should happen for everyone if they are high intensity D's.

I – Influencer

• People who have an I style are outgoing and people orientated. These styles tend to be Inspirational, Interactive, Innovators, Interested and of course Influencers. Their approach will be fast paced and optimistic. They will be motivated by gaining recognition, being upbeat and having fun. Kool and the Gang's 'Celebrate good times' being the only place to be for a high I.

• I's have real strengths around persuading, enthusing and motivating others. They are great at identifying the 'who' and will want to know who is going to be involved. They like incentives and generating enthusiasm to succeed. I's nevertheless can have a number of key weaknesses, such as being impulsive and overly optimistic at times. Think about the George Ezra lyrics 'Give me one good reason why I should never make a change.' I's need reasons 'not' to change. Due to their need for fast paced and innovative environments these styles can be on to the next thing before you know it, and so at times can lack follow through. They fear a loss of popularity.

- As a leader I's tend to be motivational and energising, they like positivity and change, and are likely to communicate through 'selling' the benefit of something to others. They are likely to be highly interactive and animated if they are high intensity I's.

S – Steadiness

- People who have an S style are more reserved and people orientated. These styles tend to be Supportive, Sincere, Stable and Security or Status-Quo driven. They will be motivated by gaining appreciation and acceptance. Their approach will be steady paced and seeking harmony.

- S's have real strengths around creating a sense of wellbeing for the team. There motto is likely to be the great Musketeer's refrain 'All for one and one for all.' They are great listeners and reflectors. These styles want to know we are doing the right thing. They are patient, loyal, practical and highly supportive. S's nevertheless can have a number of key weaknesses, such as being slow to act through indecision, being worrisome and at times being too self-sacrificing. Think about The Three Degrees plea 'When will I see you again?' Due to their fear of the loss of security these styles can slow all the processes down.

- As a leader S's tend to be inclusive and affirmative, they like consistency and a sense of calmness, and are likely to communicate through listening and consultation. They are likely to be highly change averse if they are high intensity S's.

C – Conscientious

- People who have a C style are more reserved and task orientated. These styles tend to be Competent, Careful and Concerned Critical thinkers, and of course Conscientious. They will be motivated by the pursuit of excellence and doing things right. Their approach will be to follow clearly defined systems and procedures.

- C's have real strengths around paying attention to quality, standards, accuracy and the detail. They are great planners, thorough, organized and doggedly persistent logical thinkers. These people are definitely not gamblers. As Kenny Rogers sang 'You've got to know when to hold 'em, Know when to fold 'em, Know when to walk away, Know when to run.' C's nevertheless can have a number of key weaknesses, such as being overly Critical and hard to please perfectionists who can get stuck in paralysis by analysis through their fear of getting things wrong and receiving criticism without validation.

- As a leader C's tend to be deliberate and enforcers of the rule. They like self-discipline and compliance, and are likely to communicate through the written word (email) with highly detailed instructions. They are likely to be driven solely by facts and data if they are high intensity C's.

Self-reflection

You might like to take a moment to consider the four personality styles noted above.

- Which of these motivations, approaches, strengths, weaknesses and fears relate to you?
- What might this mean for you, and your interactions with

others?

It is interesting that during my researches individual personality was seen to dictate the culture desired and the culture individuals try to transmit:

Cultures

- *D culture of responsibility and high standards,*
- *I culture of inclusiveness, positivity, engagement and recognition,*
- *S culture that is participatory, consultative (and need for high levels of self-awareness at senior level),*
- *C culture being an ordered system.*

Transmitters

- *D's lead by example and take responsibility,*
- *I's have regular team meetings, informal and formal feedback, talk not email,*
- *S's create good working relationships through trust and support, being accessible and approachable,*
- *C's ensure sound systems and structures approach.*

Blends

Before progressing it is worth taking some time for a short overview of the key blends to better understand how people with one dominant and one secondary style are more likely to behave, and to review where the most likely areas of conflict might arise.

Key blends are likely to be:

- Dominant/ Influencer – D/I or I/D
- Influencer/ Steady – I/S or S/I
- Steady/ Conscientious – S/C or C/S
- Conscientious/ Dominant – C/D or D/C

Dominant/ Influencer – D/I or I/D

- People who have a D/I or I/D style are likely to be fast paced, bold and optimistic. These styles are likely to have high levels of passion in what they do and will be able to inspire others to join them. These styles are often described as charismatic. However, if they get out of control they can be impulsive and aggressive. They fear loss of power and loss of attention.

Influencer/ Steady – I/S or S/I

- People who have an I/S or S/I style are likely to be friendly, positive and respectful of others contributions. These styles are likely to have high level of empathy, patience and will look to build close friendships and relationships. These styles are often described as affirming. However, if they do not keep control they can be slow to address underperformance through their aversion to conflict. They fear aggression and being disliked.

Steady/ Conscientious – S/C or C/S

- People who have an S/C or C/S style are likely to be fair minded, methodical and consistent. These styles are likely to have an even temperament, use diplomacy and be very practical. However, if they do not keep control they can become rigid, get bogged down in the detail, become indecisive and withdraw due to their fear of emotionally charged situations and ambiguity.

Conscientious/ Dominant – C/D or D/C

- People who have a C/D or D/C style are likely to be determined, logical and results orientated. These styles are likely to be fairly blunt in their approach and seek high standards from themselves and from others. They are likely to be highly competent and seek out inefficiencies.

However, if they get out of control they can become highly insensitive, put a negative spin on everything, and become cynical and critical. They fear failure and a lack of control.

Complimentary and the potential for conflict

The most obvious potential for conflict would be between task and people styles, or between the fast paced outgoing styles and the slower paced more reserved styles. The extremes are likely to be high intensity D's and S's, or high intensity I's and C's.

D's and S's gravitate and repel;

- D's like to lead and exude confidence, S's like the security this offers.
- But D's can see S's as inflexible and slow, and S's can see D's as dogmatic bullies.

I's and C's gravitate and repel;

- I's like to make things fun and so can lighten up the lives of serious C's.
- But I's can see C's as overly negative know it all's, and C's can see I's as impulsive show offs.

This is something I have experienced myself, as a high I, having worked extensively with high C's. My natural inclination is to get bored with the detail, irritated by pedantry, frustrated by perceived negativity and stifled by a general lack of fun. DISC has really opened my eyes to my own patterns of behavior and the behaviors in others that habitually annoy me, as well as really clarifying the key strengths and weaknesses all personality types bring to the table. This has significantly raised my self-awareness and other-awareness and given me a much greater sense of compassion that has transformed my interpersonal relationships, especially with people who show high intensity C traits.

Indeed, DISC has been invaluable in my realization of the need for me to lift my own C trait in writing this book where a high degree of organization and planning is required.

Self-reflection

- Now that you know a bit more about DISC and the blends, take a moment to consider which of these most resonate with you. Jot down any thoughts, or points for further consideration.
- Who do you know that you don't see eye to eye with? Jot down any thoughts you have about this person's potential style.
    - What are the key strengths this person brings to the situation, team or business?
    - How might you better communicate with this person now to enable better interrelationships?

Having looked at a few core concepts (values, beliefs, purpose, culture and leadership) and an overview of DISC, you might find it insightful to return to these sections and do, what **Bev James** in *DO IT! OR DITCH IT* termed, the DISC Walk. This is where you think through each of these concepts from the perspective of each of the four main personality styles.

- What would a D think?
- What would an I think?
- What would an S think?
- What would a C think?

This will allow you to see things from a different perspective. It will also enable you to understand better how others might view values, beliefs, purpose, culture and your leadership style. From doing this you should get a more holistic view of what drives you and the messages you are communicating.

In summation then it seems to me that to a great extent our values and beliefs are inherited through our various cultural settings, initially the family and then our peer groups, through the process of socialization. This whole socialization process though is driven by our prevailing hegemonic stance. If we want to challenge who we are, what our values and our purpose could be, the choices we have, and the drivers for our businesses we need to be willing to challenge this hegemony through first and foremost transforming ourselves.

Our individual personality is initially shaped through a combination of biological and psychological factors. Combined this could lead to a position of distressed determinism. However, what is equally clear to me is that while our personality cannot be fundamentally changed it can be managed or mismanaged and our values and beliefs can be questioned. In light of the fact that culture contributes to (if not shapes) the development of our values and beliefs, and culture itself is no more than an invented reality, this means our values and beliefs which we invariable consider as fixed are in-fact also no less invented. And as a consequence, can be reinvented. The positive and productive personalities and cultures sought can then emerge and soar to that 'birds-eye view' Colin Wilson advocates that will allow us individually and collectively to embrace our 'yes' to life.

"Post. Mail. News of the World. Post. Mail. News of the World. Post. Mail. News of the World."

This is my mantra as I trudge to the shops to buy the Sunday papers for my step-father; a conflicted journey.

"Why can't he go and buy his own papers?" I complain to my Mum.

"Just go and do what you're told. Do what you are told," is her mantra back. Yet another nail in my abandonment coffin.

My step-father is the focus for my unresolved frustration and anger; has been since my Mum and my Dad separated.

My step-father's passion is football and I hate football.

In fact I've always hated football but that had never been an issue until after the divorce and the move to another town and a new school where football was what 'all the boys did.'

Except me.

"Forgot your kit again, Adams!" came the gleeful quip from Mr. Butch my PE teacher. "Right, stand in line."

I would continually 'forget' my football kit which would result in me standing in line for the 'belt' every session for the entire first year at secondary school.

You have to remember in those days' physical punishment was allowed.

Nay, not allowed; encouraged, savored and for some an art form. The three worst culprits were.

Mr. Test-tube in science, who would make us cross our fingers so he could belt the most tender of areas.

Mr. No-Calculators-Allowed in maths, who would jump to great heights to garner as much force behind his punishments as he could muster.

And of course Mr Butch, who would rush at it with lots of little sharp jabs.

Very different approaches that did little to galvanize my love for either of their subjects.

I had often been termed 'sensitive' which didn't seem to affect my gregariousness and lively interest in others. Until, that is, the blind-eye of these very same teachers to the bullying I was experiencing on a daily basis at the hands of my new class 'mates' pushed me into the introverted world of Marvel and DC comics.

So, on the way for the Sunday papers, regurgitating my mantra, I would also be contemplating my next comic offerings.

And so it was that the Post. Mail. News of the World came to be my mantra that acted as a focus for my growing impotent rage and sense of powerlessness. This I believe set my beliefs (which became my limiting beliefs) that reshaped how I mismanaged my own personality for years to come allowing my 'shadow self' full reign.

I will elaborate on the nature of archetypes and shadow selves in section T.

Part Two

A to Z

So let us now take our A to Z journey and see how this can help you in taking a more appropriate approach to making effective decisions, taking effective action, through effective interactions with other people, to cultivate positive and productive cultures for your lives that will enable you to succeed in achieving or exceeding your desired goals.

As we progress through our A to Z journey I will make some references to my A to Z Framework and its relevant sub-models. These will be fully articulated in the subsequent 'Pulling it all together' section. First though, let's skip to the end.

Being able to articulate my own purpose was a fundamental gap when I started this book. I am now clear that my purpose is to be the 'I' in the crowd. By this I mean, use my learning to support others to change positively.

My A to Z Framework and its sub-models are the means by which I believe I can do that in a way that will inspire you and ensure that I am inspired by you. My framework looks to solve five key problems, in order to be able to cultivate positive and productive cultures. These are:

1   Knowing your 'default' traits as your starting point.
2   Knowing yourself and self-mastery.
3   Knowing your why and how to influence others.
4   Knowing your sticking points and moving on.
5   Knowing your energy flow and sustaining success.

The A to Z Framework offers a stepping stone approach to addressing and solving these problems, with **DISC personality profiling** as your starting point. The most important aspect though will be your own learning points as you progress through the A to Z journey with me.

Chapter One

A - Affirmative and Adaptive Cultures

The philosopher Herbert Marcuse says, in *The Affirmative Character of Culture*, that an affirmative culture has 'right on its side.' This must be good news then for everyone out there with an affirmative 'default' leadership style.

Affirmative leaders tend to have key strengths around being positive like having an open-door policy, showing empathy, building a sense of loyalty through praise and acknowledgment of others contributions. These are great attributes for building successful teams.

There is much to learn from the example of affirmative leaders. Especially for those leaders who are more 'resolute' or 'commanding.' Simple things, like:

- saying 'thank you',
- watching your facial expressions – especially those judgmental looks,
- saying 'good morning',
- and taking the time to give other pleasant greetings.

David Petraeus, retired four-star general and former director of the Central Intelligence Agency describes an affirmative model of leadership, founded on an assumption that the vast majority of people want to do the best that they can, as one that "inspires those an individual lead to do just that, to do their best to 'be all that they can be.' It's a style or approach that's very conscious in conveying a respect for the individual … and that conveys that the leader looks forward to confirming the excellence of those he is privileged to lead."

Research clearly shows that productivity increases and turnover rates decrease the more affirmative traits the leader shows.

So it's all good news then?

Well, unfortunately not. Before we go patting ourselves on the back too much we might want to consider that all default settings blind us to other approaches. DISC personality profiling has much to offer here in directing our thinking around effective leadership and default styles. Whether you are a D (Dominant), I (Influencer), S (Steady) or C (Conscientious), or more likely a 'blend' of two or more of these personality traits, you will already have identified some of your own key strengths and weaknesses. But with heightened levels of self-awareness these can be greatly refined to ensure a broader field of leadership responses and approaches.

It is not uncommon, due to their need for harmony, for high affirmative leaders to be slow to address conflict situations and underperformance which can then spiral out of control resulting in a culture of aggression or underachievement. The very opposite of what they were aiming for.

An example of this from my own experience was when I was brought in as a consultant to work with a highly affirmative senior manager whose department had just been inspected by Ofsted and judged to 'require improvement.' Initially the lead team had assumed the issue to be one of insufficiently good teachers which could be quickly turned around through a suite of CPD events and some new blood. It didn't take long though before the real issues came bubbling to the surface; a senior manager who wouldn't address performance management issues that led to a split between those who 'played the game' and those who had to pick up the shortfall, resulting in back biting and a loss of focus on the needs of the learners; and a lack of Governance scrutiny that had allowed this situation to escalate.

So affirmative leaders need to learn a thing or two from their 'resolute' or 'commanding' peers around challenge and pace. What does this mean practically? For a high 'affirmative' leader the key learning points are;

- to take control and draw that line in the sand,
- accept and see the flaws in others,
- hold people to account,
- meet resistance head on,
- seek out inefficiencies,
- and accept that 'good enough' is not always good enough.

So while Marcuse may be correct in his assertion that affirmative culture has 'right on its side', this is only half the story for an affirmative leader. The practical implications for the business or organization of an affirmative leader taking on board the key learning points noted above is immense when matched to their natural people orientated approach. This is the real strength Petraeus describes when he matches adaptive to affirmative leadership.

In my experience and through the direct research carried out for this book I found very little recognition around the need for 'adaptive' practices. Likewise, there appears to be a lack of understanding or belief in any real ability individuals have to impact on the prevailing culture, let alone cultivate the culture one might desire. In the minds of most leaders and managers I've spoken to culture shapes individuals but individuals (other than the leader) do not impact on the prevailing culture.

This more than anything has emphasized for me the need for more clarity and greater understanding of culture and cultural culti-vation at all levels, including at the most senior level, and therefore the benefit of adaptive practices.

So how do we develop an understanding of our 'default' leadership styles and how do we adapt our styles to the requirements of the situation? In short, through the development of self-awareness.

Research shows that while people join an organization, they leave their managers. To minimize conflict, reduce wastage through high turnover and so missed potential for the profitability of your business we (as leaders) need to build our levels of self-awareness (the practical steps to this will be discussed later in this book, in section M).

Self-reflection

In the meantime, here are a few useful questions you might like to ask yourself as an individual and as a leader:

- Am I trusted by others?
- Am I sensitive to the needs of others?
- Am I aware of the impact I have on others?
- Do I encourage people to be candid with me without worry of repercussions?

An affirmative culture then is the key platform in which to build from, but insufficient on its own to cover all eventualities. For this we require an adaptive stance. Adaptiveness however can only be effective if derived at from a position of self-awareness that better directs your own actions within a given situation. This resonates well with myself and a comparison between two situations might illustrate this point well:

Situation One

I had taken over the quality department in a college early on in my career. Issues had been identified around a member of the quality team. I had been informed she was 'not up to the job' but no one to date had taken responsibility for dealing with the issue. I started with an affirmative approach; laid out my expectations and that staff would want to reach those expectations, put into place training and support mechanisms, and monitored the situation. Nothing changed and so I reiterated my expectations, laid on more training and heightened our one-to-one support sessions. Nothing changed. I reiterated... By now the rest of the team's underlying frustrations had surfaced. Tensions had risen. Sniping was the order of the day. Sickness levels rose and work suffered overall. And I reiterated...

Situation Two

I had taken over the role of Director of the business facing department at a large college. The department was underperforming against income targets, learner success rates and was no longer a financially viable entity. My naturally affirmative and people orientated approach came to the fore as I brought the staff together to better understand what had gone wrong. On the one hand I could see a level of frustration in a naturally 'selling' team - leaders who had been forced to stay office bound to manage the team. This changed and she became the key externally facing partnership manager. And on the other hand I could see a level of disengagement from a number of staff who no longer had any bond with the organization. I now recognized the need to address this quickly and that my natural 'default' affirmative position was not called for here. I set up speedy HR intervention that resulted in these staff being managed out of the organization and replaced by new, fresh and enthusiastic staff. The result being increased business, improved success for learners, subsequent repeat business, enhanced referrals and a department that was financially viable within the year.

Knowing your default approach and having the self-awareness

to understand when this default approach is appropriate and when not, I now believe, is the fundamental starting point for decisions around cultivating the positive and productive cultures we wish to immerse ourselves in. This therefore is the basis from which my A to Z Framework builds.

My key learning point:

I had taken on an affirmative stance when I was younger as a means to convince my Mum everything would be 'ok.' Although I now see this was really done as a way of getting her attention and recognition for myself.

We need to know our 'default' approach from which to adapt to suit current and changing needs.

What is your key learning point?

_____

_____

_____

_____

_____

_____

Chapter Two

B - Buddhist Cultures

I 'don't know' can be a frightening concept, yet these are the most important words in Buddhism. For Buddhists 'don't know' is an exciting place to be. This is the place of great focus and potentiality. Keeping 'don't know' in mind brings us back to our 'beginners' mind where we can better focus on 'just doing', so when we are eating we just eat, when we are walking we just walk, when we are working we just work and when we are listening we just listen.

'Don't know' warns us not to be limited by what we think we already know.

From a Western perspective we often see 'don't know' as a weakness, an absence of knowledge, or philosophically a question of knowledge;

- What do we know?
- Who is this 'we' who thinks they know?
- Why do we need to know?
- How do we know it?

Whichever of these questions most resonates with you will indicate a preferred way of looking at things. This in turn will indicate your 'default' personality trait - whether that be Dominant, Influencer, Steady or Conscientious. The implication of this default personality trait when we are in a 'don't know' position can be profound.

For a high D

Dominant personalities tend to have a need to be in charge, so not knowing can appear to undermine their position of authority.

A useful response here might be "Based on what we know now; my thoughts are..."

A 'don't know' response from others can appear to a D as a blockage and not solutions focused. 'Don't know' will almost certainly be seen as impacting negatively on the bottom-line, but actually offers a great opportunity for challenge (as well as the potential for failure).

For a high I

Influencer personalities tend to have a need for recognition, so not knowing can be a difficult or exciting place to be, one that might lead to a loss of popularity if they do not have the required knowledge, or the opportunity for great innovation.

A useful response here might be "Lets brainstorm."

A 'don't know' response from others can appear to an I as too negative. 'Don't know' could come across as impacting negatively on the enthusiasm of the team, but offers great opportunities for incentives and the fun of new learning and exploration.

For a high S

Steady personalities tend to have a need for security, so not knowing can appear to upset the established harmony.

A useful response here might be "Let's reflect on the options."

A 'don't know' response from others could appear to an S as

confrontational and not team orientated. 'Don't know' might also be seen as impacting negatively on the traditional way of doing things, but offers great opportunities for collaboration (while raising the potential for unease and insecurity).

For a high C

Conscientious personalities tend to have a need for clearly defined explanations, so not knowing can appear to undermine their position in knowing and being right.

A useful response here might be "I don't currently have that information to hand. I'll find out."

A 'don't know' response from others could appear to a C as sloppy and lacking in detail. 'Don't know' will almost certainly be seen as impacting negatively on quality and being able to do things right, but offers great opportunities for future planning and working out the proper way to do something (while also raising the fear of risk taking and making mistakes).

Uncertainty, ambiguity and being stuck

Lots of research has been carried out around the issues of uncertainty and ambiguity, and especially how leaders respond in situations of uncertainty and ambiguity; of not knowing. You only have to think about Jerry Rhodes 'Effective Intelligence', John Holland's work on 'Complex Adaptive Systems', David Snowden's work using the 'Cynefin Framework', or Ralph Stacey's 'Model of Uncertainty' to name but a few.

The perceptions of uncertainty, the ability to deal with different levels of ambiguity and the degree to which individuals and groups show uncertainty avoidance will differ, partly due to personality and partly due to individual and group learned experiences; all of which can be learned, unlearned, transferred and reinforced. What is certain though is the difficulties many find when faced with uncertainty (we will elaborate on this aspect in section F) and yet as Charles Sheen said,

"Uncertainty is a sign of humility, and humility is just the ability or the willingness to learn."

It might be worth asking yourself at this point; What do you do when you or your team 'don't know' what the next step in your life or for your business should be?

One of the key issues for a place of uncertainty and 'I don't know' is the accompanying feeling of being 'stuck.' This can vary from being stuck in the same old rut, working in the same old ways, with the same old people, and the same old problems. Or it might be stuck because you are confronted with new ways of doing things, new approaches, new people who expect things done differently, new problems. The two most common ways of dealing with being stuck is to take a fight or flight approach;

1 To attack it head on. Any action is better than no action approach that too often results in misdirection, loss of focus, energy and resources that can lead to competitor advantage, or financial ruin for you as an individual or the business.

2 To avoid the issue. The old sticking your head in the sand and hope it goes away approach that too often results in personal and business stagnation and decline.

As creatures of habit being stuck can actually be relatively comfortable for many people, especially when accompanied with a feeling of 'I do know.' But unless we expand our field of comfort through the occasional stretch and challenge our comfort zone soon becomes our prison zone. Our habits become our limiting beliefs (as we discussed in the Introduction) and our successes can only ever be fixed in a static environment and more likely declining in a changing dynamic business setting.

But what do we mean by this term 'comfort zone'?

If we consider the illustrations below we can see that our comfort zone is the central zone we spend most of our lives in. This is both our auto-response and safety zone. Most of our lives are spent in automatic pilot where we do not need to think but can do most things unconsciously. However, we can consciously choose to step outside this zone, into what is called our stretch zone. This can be seen as the place where things are more challenging and as the place where we feel more alive and exhilarated. What sits outside the stretch zone is the panic zone. This is where we are likely to freeze up or go into melt down. This is a frightening place to be, not merely challenging. The trick is to expand your comfort zone bit by bit in order that we continuously increase our potential and our performance.

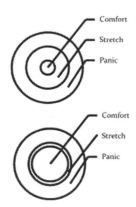

This process increases what is in our comfort zone and pushes our stretch zone to the limits of our panic zone, so what initially would have panicked us begins to take on a less threatening aspect and becomes simply a stretch and challenge.

I was working with a company that had gone through a merger due to rationalization and efficiency savings. As a consequence, a number of staff had been 'slotted' into roles they neither desired nor felt they had the skills base required to perform successfully. One example was of an Account Manager, a highly people orientated person in an external facing role, who had been slotted into the role of an Operations Manager, a technical and task orientated role. For the individual member of staff this allowed for a sense of security in retaining a post, but quickly turned to a lack of fulfillment, doubts and an eventual loss in confidence in his own abilities. He felt 'stuck' in the role and in his career within the company. He 'didn't know' how to extract himself from the situation without putting his job, salary and security at risk. Yet he was aware of the potential consequences of not performing well enough in his new role.

It was at this point the manager had been referred to myself for coaching. We broke the situation into discrete chunks in order to find the steps that would allow the client to become 'unstuck.' The chunks centered around fear in his new role, perceived lack of skills, challenges around change, a growing lack of confidence and mounting limiting beliefs. We focused on two key areas:

- *Stretch and challenge, and realistic expectations.*
- *Imagined reality, and reframing of limiting beliefs.*

This then allowed the client to act in a more constructive and effective manner that enabled him to expand his field of comfort, and indeed led to the client progressing onto a stage of enhanced energy and experiencing what for him was his first 'peak experience.'

My key learning point:

I had spent much of my early years in a state of 'don't know' (why did my Mum and Dad split up? why did she abandon me? why did she put up with my step-father's tantrums and punches? why couldn't I convince her to leave?). Without answers it became easier to shut off, distance myself and build around me a state of certainty on what 'I did know.'

We need to expand our field of comfort through stretch and challenge or our comfort zone soon becomes our prison zone.

What is your key learning point?

Chapter Three

C - Creative Cultures

In light of the previous sections concerns around I don't know, it might be worth reflecting on the nature of creativity and innovation which start from an initial premise of 'don't know'; a question to be answered, or a problem to be solved. It might also be worth reminding ourselves, as Ralph Stacey put it, "Systems are capable of variety and novelty only when they are pushed far from equilibrium...keeping a system in orderly equilibrium is the same as trapping it in endless repetition of its past and destroying its creativity."

Changes in markets and the competitive strategies of large organizations have increased the pressure on SMEs to focus on innovation, innovation capabilities and innovation management as the key driver of growth and business success. Yet at the same time there has been a fixation on quantitative targets which emphasize what can be easily measured.

Where things are more difficult to measure the effect on such a system can have negative consequences. Teresa Amabile in *'How to kill creativity'* suggests that it is impossible to work creatively towards a target that keeps moving, so stability over a meaningful period of time is required. Building creativity is a slow process. It takes time. There is a need to allocate time for exploration and incubation, and there is a growing recognition that organizations need both innovation and implementation; too much of one can lead to innovation fatigue, while too much of the other leads back to an obsession with accountability and compliance. This gives us a more nuanced understanding of the need for a balance between the outgoing, fast paced change drivers and the more reserved, slower paced status quo drivers. This is an important point for leaders to consider, especially leaders who are currently driving their businesses or organizations from a fixed 'default' position.

When dealing with issues of uncertainty, complexity and multiple demands in either a coaching or consultancy capacity a good starting point is usually the Circle of Life or Progress Wheel. This can either focus on the 'tasks', using the GROW model and traditional time-management approaches, or focus on the underlying issues around confidence, esteem and beliefs through reframing, visualization and working on core values to transcend limiting beliefs.

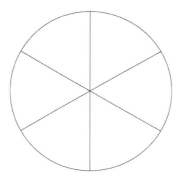

Circle of Life or Progress Wheel – identify the key aspects to be worked on. This is usually a minimum of six separate issues, but certainly no more than twelve or you are likely to lose focus.

It is widely recognized that autonomy is important for driving innovation, as this fosters intrinsic motivation and a sense of ownership. Managers however invariably mismanage freedom through frequently changing goals, or having poorly defined goals, or through granting autonomy in name only within a proscribed process.

A culture then that has driven the need for innovation is the very culture that has the potential to kill creativity.

The whole notion of complexity has taken on great significant these days, especially in relation to neuroscience and what is known as complex adaptive systems. This has profound implications for organizational development and especially team working and consensus building. There is a true recognition now of how complex and so how unpredictable we can be as people and so as staff, as managers, and as leaders. We can choose to follow or ignore the rules. We can choose to make new rules. We can choose to work together or create disharmony. Therefore, getting consensus and ensuring all staff are moving in the same direction with the same goal can be seen as almost impossible. Yet, as we mentioned when discussing DISC personality profiling people tend to have predictable patterns of behavior and so tend to be unpredictable in predictable ways or situations. The more unconscious we are of our patterns of behavior the more predictable we are likely to be. The more conscious (aware) we are of our patterns the more readily we can disrupt (or adapt) them.

What is so fascinating is the notion of 'emergence' which has been defined by Kevin Mihata in his essay The Persistence of Emergence as "the process by which patterns or global-level structures arise from interactive local-level processes. This 'structure' or 'pattern' cannot be understood or predicted from the behavior or properties of the component units alone." This means that emergence cannot be planned or predicted, but is nevertheless not random either. Emergence is considered by many as the basis for creativity and innovation. Indeed, Richard Seel in his book Emergence in Organizations has come up with a list of pre-conditions for the cultivation of emergence. Seel writes "If the conversations are rich, diverse and unconstrained there is the possibility of creative and adaptive change. If not, the organization will be doomed to repeat itself until it is so far out of alignment with its environment that it will die."

Culture revisited

We have mentioned over and over the term 'culture', so to remind ourselves what we really mean by this. Culture has something to do with cumulative, collective and time-bound behavior that has been learnt through repetition. Patterns of behavior (i.e. our practices) that convey our values; units of imitation (what are called 'memes'). The core of a culture is formed by its values, whether the values are explicitly understood or not.

Let's expand a bit on organizational culture. Gerrit Broekstra suggested in *Metaphor and the Evolution of the living organization* that we are moving into a new paradigm about organization and management, called the evolutionary paradigm, which is associated with the metaphor of the brain. By this Broekstra meant a 'complex dynamic system poised at the edge of order and chaos.' This has now been reaffirmed through the recent work in neuroscience and leadership as noted above (see *Neuroscience for Leadership* for a good overview).

The prevailing managerial ideology Broekstra believes is still 'doing things right' rather than 'doing the right thing', efficiency orientated rather than effectiveness (system thinking). This reflects Stephen Covey's thinking in his hugely influential book 'The 7 Habits of Highly Effective People.' The new science of complexity has been used to offer insights into the evolution of organizations and management paradigms; from mechanistic, to organismic and then to evolutionary, which correspond to the metaphors of; the machine, the organism and finally the brain (the organizational forms of; functional, divisional and network organizations).

- The oldest paradigm, mechanistic, rooted in the 19thC materialistic/reductionist worldview is still around in many organizations today (hierarchy, power distance, conformity and obsessed with vertical control). The divisional organization though can have a mechanistic approach within it, while organized according to the functional form, with autonomous business units working in entrepreneurial form to a particular product or market.

- The organismic paradigm developed from the divisional philosophy where each part adapts to its particular environment, which could result in some parts in a stable environment becoming mechanistic, while others in less predictable environments could become more organic. This is more effectiveness-orientated but with the view that the environment was a given concrete entity. The network form is characterised by complexity, innovation, out-sourcing, collaboration and a search for synergy.

- The evolutionary paradigm recognizes the new science of complexity and organizations as living systems. The motivation behind this is for the network organization to provide stimulation for innovation. Connectionism, from cognitive science, has led to the brain metaphor. There are similarities between the evolution of the brain and organizational forms, such as reptilian, to limbic, to neocortex. Creative intelligence does not sit with senior leadership but is distributed throughout the entire organization, like a neural network.

While the first two organizational paradigms can be seen as fragmented, it is encouraging to think a more holistic networked organization could result in a 'coherence in corporate consciousness' resulting in creativity, innovation and synergy. This connects well with Travis Bradberry's thinking around leadership having to do with 'social influence which maximizes the efforts of others toward the achievement of a greater good.' However, making use of Jung's collective unconscious where the culture of the organization has been called the 'organizational unconscious', this could more soberingly be the cumulative, collective and time-bound behavior that has been learnt through repetition of the people working within or connected to an organization; that is, the practices that convey the true values of the organization or business, i.e. the operational values - whether consciously realized or not, as opposed to a 'truth' in 'reality' (remember earlier we discussed the two types of values; idealistic and operational).

If we consider for a minute Charles Handy's notion of four cultures in his seminal book *Understanding Organizations*, we can better see the connection between cumulative behavior and practices and how these convey the personality of the organization (although it is unlikely Handy would have put it this way).

- Handy talks about the Power culture which is led by an all-powerful figurehead, conveyed as Zeus, who rules by whim and impulse. In this organization there will be few rules and little in the way of bureaucracy. The balance of influence will dictate decisions and the organization will be highly responsive. However, there is likely to be a tough and abrasive approach. This conveys a decidedly D/I personality style.

- We also have the Task culture which is a matrix organization that is based on the customer always being right. This organization is very team orientated with a sense of the whole being greater than the sum of the parts. The. organization can also be very quick moving which gives a sense of a blended I/S personality style.

- The Person culture is a listening culture. Here individual people are central to the decision-making process, and individuals do what they are good at. This conveys a real sense of an S personality style. In Handy's opinion this organizational culture does not last very long and is invariably replaced before long by one of the other three.

- And then the Role culture which is led by Apollo the God of Reason. Here bureaucracy runs rife. Procedures and rules drive the approach, where efficiency is the byword for stability. In this organization everyone has a designated function and specialism. This conveys a real sense of a C personality style. However, this kind of organization, while solid in stable times, is slow to change and can crash in more ambiguous and complex times.

What this shows us is that our image of organizational cultures is still fairly limited to the mechanistic and organismic paradigms. The current operational values base of many organizations still need significantly shifting if we want to move from a command and control ethos to fully embracing a networked and distributed future.

Remember: culture is an imagined reality. It might therefore be time to put aside our Western fear of not-knowing and truly cultivate a culture that supports personal and business growth.

However, on a more positive note although cultures appear to have set values, beliefs and norms of approach when seen as a snap shot or over time, they are actually in a constant state of flux. This flux is driven primarily by our own internal contradictions (which we will discuss at greater lengths in section T). It is these contradictions, although we tend to dislike uncertainty and ambiguity as noted earlier, that nevertheless fuel change. Indeed, as Yuval Noah Harari stated in his book *Sapiens: A Brief History of*

Humankind, "Once cultures appear, they never ceased to change and develop." This allows for new possibilities and high levels of complexity.

Self-reflection

- You might want to reflect on the following questions;
- What is your strategy for cultivating the culture you want in your organization, business or life?
- Does this include supporting the development of creativity and innovation?
- Does this reflect where you or your business currently are?
- How do you know?

My key learning point:

As I grew older 'leakage' led me to know there was more; more to my past, my current approach and so to my future potential. But I was too locked in to what 'I knew' to know what to do about it.

We need to embrace complexity if we want to survive and thrive.

What is your key learning point?

_____

_____

_____

_____

_____

Chapter Four

D - Diverse Cultures

You might have heard about the rise of the 'Mannies' over the recent years and the benefit this has on childcare and for society as a whole. Male nannies allow us all to see a different side to childcare, male domains and expectations, to question societal stereotypes, and our own perceptions and career aspirations.

Stereotyping is a form of shorthand that easily masks limited thinking or limiting beliefs. From an historical cultural perspective, they are part of the 'vicious cycle' of chance historical situations that have become rigid social systems.

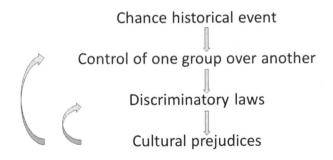

Chance historical event

Control of one group over another

Discriminatory laws

Cultural prejudices

Tim Cook, CEO of Apple, stated in a 2013 tweet Workplace Equality Is Good for Business, "Long before I started work as the CEO of Apple, I became aware of a fundamental truth: People are much more willing to give of themselves when they feel that their selves are being fully recognized and embraced."

Equality and diversity is all about creating a fairer society where we recognize and celebrate difference. More so it is about celebrating what those differences can bring and add to all our contributions to society. It's about empowering everyone. If we think back to our last section, we can see that diversity is a key part in the development of 'emergence' that allows for creativity and innovation – essential if you want your business to survive and thrive in the future.

The main philosophical drivers for recognising equality and diversity have been 'Identity Politics, or Politics of Recognition', i.e. questioning our sameness and difference on the one hand, and 'Politics of Redistribution', i.e. resources and economics on the other. An attempt to bring together 'politics of recognition and redistribution' has led to what we now call the nine 'protected characteristics' – age, disability, gender, gender reassignment, marriage and civil partnership, pregnancy or maternity, race, religion or belief, sexual orientation – wrapped around economic disadvantage, as exemplified by the Equality Act 2010.

In theory The Equality Act 2010 covers most aspects of employment and recruitment, although there are still many examples of inequality at work, such as;

- the pay differential between men and women,
- the polarisation of high and low wage employment,
- the pay gap between the over-50s and under-21s which has mushroomed by 50% in the past 15 years,
- ethnic minority groups - even with higher levels of education - experience lower employment rates than their White counterparts,
- people with a declared disability who are 50% less likely to be in employment,
- and of course the north/ south divide that we read about daily in the local press (up north anyway).

And yet diversity in society has impacted greatly in many areas of our lives, such as the food we eat, the clothes we wear, the art we appreciate and the journeys and holidays that have been opened up to us. The greatest consequences of diversity in society is that it brings us into contact with new ideas, new ways of seeing things and new ways of thinking, and so enables us to challenge our own beliefs and prejudices. Indeed, without this challenge to beliefs that have become 'limiting' society would stagnate – as would your business. (It might be worth reflecting back on your own and your businesses limiting beliefs we discussed during the Introduction section, especially in light of the learning from section C.)

There are a number of key benefits to business's who promote and truly embrace equality and diversity. One key benefit of equality and diversity within the workplace is similar to the saying 'the whole is greater than the sum of the parts' where the business as a whole is enhanced through the pooling of individual and collective resources.

Another benefit of having a diverse workforce is attracting and retaining the best people for the job. This is a real boon to team working where having a diverse range of skills, experiences and knowledge base creates opportunities to generate and build on new and varied ideas. Connected to this point, a diverse workforce enhances your bottom-line. With a diverse workforce you will more readily appeal to a diverse customer base, have internal understating and specialist knowledge of your customers and new and potential customers, giving you that competitive edge and potential for greater market share (especially important as you progress towards international markets).

From a purely pragmatic perspective a benefit to having a diverse workforce is avoiding potential legal threats and costs. Being proactive in your equality and diversity policies and procedures can reduce the likelihood of discrimination and so complaints, legal investigations and the potential of fines and reputational damage through bad press.

The reputational aspect of having a diverse workforce therefore is a major benefit as it touches on all the aspects already mentioned. You will attract and retain more talented staff, thereby impacting on your bottom-line, give you the cutting edge to generate new markets or strengthen existing market loyalty, generating profit and reducing costs associated with discriminatory workplaces.

Key fact - 76% of businesses see reputation as an important driver of business behavior in relation to equality and diversity.

There has been much political and philosophical debate around protective characteristics within the context of economic disadvantage – which some see as a return to a deficit mode based on victim mentality, while others see this as evidence that redistribution has taken precedence over recognition. To move beyond this polarized view, we need to promote good working relationships and partnerships that foster learning at strategic and individual levels. This is usually referred to as Community Cohesion and Social Inclusion which is about linking communities, the promotion of digital inclusion, respecting different backgrounds, and primarily about knowing your customer or client to better address their needs.

When we consider that marketing research shows us that in Britain alone women make the most consumer decisions. People over 50 hold 80% of the wealth of Britain. The disposable spending power of black and minority ethnic groups is estimated to be worth £32bn. And that businesses lost £60m last year due to disabled people not being able to access commercial premises or use their services. Businesses need to consider how best to tap into these markets without overtly targeting any one group. There are strong connections here with the notion of corporate consciousness and what has recently been termed the 'quadruple bottom-line model'; profits, people, planet and sustainable progress.

Through the use of DISC you can identify your customer's

fundamental needs and drivers in mere minutes. Remember the four main personality traits; Dominant, Influencer, Steady and Conscientious? Each have key needs and motivations whether that be for success of their bottom-line, recognition and fun, consistency and doing the right thing, or paying attention to quality and standards. The trick is to tap into your customer and potential customer's key needs and drivers to ensure they want to work with you and to maintain continued loyalty. Paying attention to what motivates others will ensure you give your customers or clients what they need and secure the success of your own business.

Research has long shown that messaging is most effective when motivational rather than instructional (to avoid sounding bossy or patronizing). This is an approach that will allow your business to become really personal, freeing up time to concentrate on the day to day running of your business, and with the UK economy doubling in growth in 2014 (according to ONS) enable you to focus on your longer-term business potential. Which in turn will allow you to have a greater corporate consciousness impact.

I elaborate on motivational aspects later in section P.

So let us take a closer look at diversity and how this might help us in our progress towards cultivating the positive and productive cultures we seek.

First off, let us recognize that diversity and the notion of identity have become defining characteristics in our current time. This means we are differentiated and categorised in multiple ways so we can at one point be in the 'in-group' while in another area be part of the 'out group.' In theory this should make difference easier to conceive and more readily accepted. If only life were that simple.

We know from inter and bi-cultural studies that there are positive impacts on both cognition and behavior from having bi-cultural identities. Yet we also know through 'in group project modelling' – which measures high status and excluded groups – that members of in-groups project their characteristics onto the larger group (what is called the superordinate group). This projection then allows for discrimination against those who do not hold those characteristics. An example of this would be British people who are 'white', who then project 'white' onto the superordinate group 'British.' So anyone not 'white' cannot be 'British.'

Charles Darwin, whose family was staunchly abolitionist, had noted this tendency in relation to the human species in general. As Thomas Hayden put it, "He was disheartened to see advocates of slavery justifying their position by saying that white European humans and black African humans were not the same species." Further saying, "One of the animating thoughts in the young Darwin's mind as he set out to understand the world was his conviction that all humans were one." Being one species however does not stop us from showing a sensitivity to small differences in social status. Evolutionary psychologists show us that our ancestors found the development of large scale social inequalities psychologically damaging during the shift from hunter-gatherer to farmer. Indeed, the human species has spent over 90 percent of our existence to date living in egalitarian societies. Today though the differences are huge and getting bigger "where the global elite earn thousands of times more than those at the bottom of the economic heap." The impact of this is that what was a signal for obedience has turned into a pathology where those "at the top of the pyramid, who tend to have the most decision-making responsibility, have the least stressful lives", and to quote Gore Vidal, *"It is not enough to succeed, others must fail."* Is it so surprising the select few within our dominant groups are disinclined to embrace change? Or that there is such a slow recognition in the socialized and unconsciously patterned masses of the need for a shift back to a more egalitarian position.

What is clear is that we are socially and not wholly self-constructed and can therefore be re-constructed (or more positively, cultivated) as can our cultural setting.

While lecturing at Edinburgh College of Art back in 1992 I was asked to take on the role of Equalities Officer – first point of contact for our learners. This seemed fairly innovative. Especially for someone who at the time had only recently divulged his own 'gay' sexuality, and certainly before I had a grasp of 'queer' theory and practice.

On reflection I can see this fed nicely into my own 'personality' need for recognition and my weakness for distractions.

"I'm just like a sack of potatoes."

It amazed me what people tell you when they think you are the expert.

"I'm sure you'll learn to loosen up and enjoy yourself," I say, as if I know.

"Well no one is going to want an old sack of potatoes, are they?"

"Who told you that?" I enquire. His frown tells me all I need to know. "So, what is believing that costing you?" I ask.

His eyebrows furrow and his pupils shift from side to side, so I probe a bit further. "If you no longer had that belief, what could you do?"

And to my continued amazement, I hear all about it.

This was an experience I had with a very quiet and withdrawn young man who went on to lead the Student Union and is now a highly respected arts aficionado.

And so started the embryonic of my understanding that a coaching ethos matched to embracing diversity allows us all to grow our potential.

My key learning point:

Fear that my step-father's anger would be directed at me; fear that was further enhanced through being bullied at school, developed into a generalized fear of straight men that has held me back from embracing my own difference, my own 'I'.

We need to stop tolerating and start embracing diversity to truly capitalize on its and our potential.

What is your key learning point?

_____

_____

_____

_____

_____

_____

Chapter Five

E - Energizing Cultures

Our misunderstanding that to be in control means we must make others obey us is at the root of the command and control culture that pervades too many organizations. Yet real control comes through self-restraint and in leadership parlance, self-awareness and self-management. The real job of a leader is not to control others but to harness their energies; to excite them about the business. Indeed "energizing leaders" Professor Nita Cherry says "make it easier for people to connect their energies to the goals of their groups, organizations and communities."

There is a great story from the education sector I love. It's a Bill Rogers story of the boy in class who had been attention seeking. Bill should have sent him on some time-out, but instead had battled on. The boy jumped on the table, caught hold of the beam along the ceiling and started swinging and making baboon-like noises. The rest of the class started to hoot and holler. Bill was completely out of bananas and so said to the boy "If you're not down by the time I count to ten, I'm going to climb up and seriously tickle you."

The boy instantly dropped to the ground and said, "Oh sh*t! You're not touching me!", and ran off for some self-imposed time-out.

This is a great example of the conflict between high spirits and control. Too much control and we have arrogance and intolerance, and an inability to restrain our own behavior that might better channel this over-exuberance.

Research shows that energizing leaders are four times more influential than their peers, ensuring greatly improved performance.

They do this through their ability to encourage others to sustain their energy levels in the face of challenges, at times of change and transition, and during difficult situations. This matches well with Carol Dweck's notion of a Growth Mindset where "People can be of two minds: fixed and flexible. In a changing world, flexible is better for relationships and growth."

The theory is that there are two basic mindsets; fixed and growth. A fixed mindset is where you believe that the amount of intelligence and abilities you can have is fixed at a certain amount and no matter how hard you try you cannot exceed this amount. A growth mindset is where you believe that the amount you can know or do increases and further develops the more you learn and achieve. This necessitates hard work. But as Dweck recognized it is about more than that. It is about offering what many in the education sector will recognize as 'developmental feedback' that is matched to self-development, "Let's talk about what you've tried, and what you can try next." It is about people (whether that be learners, leaders or employees) being given responsibility, and them taking responsibility on themselves.

The question for many is, how do you develop this growth mindset in yourself or others where a fixed mindset prevails? Or as Carol Dweck herself put it, "*How can we help educators adopt a deeper, true growth mindset, one that will show in their classroom practices?* You may be surprised by my answer: Let's legitimize the fixed mindset. Let's acknowledge that (1) we're all a mixture of fixed and growth mindsets, (2) we will probably always be, and (3) if we want to move closer to a growth mindset in our thoughts and practices, we need to stay in touch with our fixed-mindset thoughts and deeds." This is a fantastic example of Fredrick Perl's notion of the Paradoxical Theory of Change which I will expand on in section S, but is fundamentally about accepting what one is before any kind of change can take place.

Within a leadership context this is about driving your own energy outwards towards the greater good, where leaders become true servants. For this to occur leaders require high levels of self-awareness and a real understanding of the dual responsibility they have in their business or organization; their specific function and role on the one hand (i.e. technical knowledge) and a generic role within the whole organization on the other around vision and direction, culture and behavior and meeting the greater needs associated with doing the right thing, especially during times of change.

However, because everyone has been through the education system to some degree or other we all feel entitled to an opinion, and usually an opinion that has a high level of 'I know' attached to it. This has taken education out of the hands of the experts and placed it into the public and political domain. Change is an ever present aspect of most businesses these days, but education is an exemplar of an industry verging on 'change-fatigue.'

"Implementing change effectively has been, and seems likely to remain, one of the main challenges facing managers."

Cornall and Maxwell made the above pronouncement in 1988 and can be seen to have made a good call. Leaders all over the globe can attest to this, and indeed some brands have made their name through embracing change as a core value. You only have to think of Apple and their 'challenging the status quo.'

Quality, which historically had been based to a great extent on consistency, has been replaced by quality improvement, which necessitates some kind of change, no matter how small. The pressure for change can be internal or external; but needs to be driven by an internal recognition that it is necessary. However, many people fear that change is now out of control and is counterproductive to effectiveness, where the balance between flexibility and stability has been lost, with many organizations facing initiative overload, multiple change and competing priorities. A 2013 global survey carried out by Strategy& found that

65% of managers who participated thought that change fatigue was the biggest obstacle to successful change management practices, and yet astonishingly 96% thought change in current cultures was needed.

'Traditional' organizational structures cannot cope with too much turbulence and uncertainty (think back to our discussion on uncertainty and ambiguity). This is a growing concern for many leading thinkers in the worlds of business, politics and academia. Especially when viewed in conjunction with the changing nature of the economy, from a 'standardized' economy to a 'customized' economy. In practice this means moving from a state of tariffs and regulations, of producing larger and larger quantities of goods at affordable prices, with a dominance of traditional industries. Organizations in the traditional vain have numerous layers of management and a large core of permanent employees. In the customized economy we see the lifting of tariffs and restrictions, where products are customized through the use of new technology. There are more knowledge based activities. In this kind of organization there are fewer layers of management, greater emphasis on horizontal networks and a recognition that the complexities of tasks require teamwork and collaboration. There will be a reliance on a smaller core of permanent employees.

It is often suggested that to counter our change-rich environment leaders need to select change priorities based on the realization that we cannot change everything all at once, and that we need to hold a balance between maintenance activities and development activities. Indeed, when we consider Stephen Covey's 7 *Habits of Highly Effective People* and his equation $E = P \times PC$ (effectiveness equals production times production capability) we might want to ponder the 7th habit of Sharpening the Saw (self-renewal and CPD) and the old favorite 'I'm too busy' – too busy sawing to spend time sharpening the saw.

When the half-life of professional knowledge is currently estimated at four years the need for renewal and CPD has never been more necessary.

Changing habits, we know is notoriously difficult. We live most of our lives on 'automatic pilot', i.e. through our default habits. For most of life this makes sense as it stops us wasting our energy focused on things that can work perfectly efficiently without too much attention. Changing habits therefore seems to be working against the flow and is certainly not to be undertaken lightly. Hence why there are so many failed New Year resolutions.

The field of neurosciences as mentioned previously has come on leaps and bounds over the last decade or so. When you match this to the developments in psychology, especially the work of Carol Dweck on Fixed and Growth mindsets we mentioned previously, we really get an understanding of the complexity of our emotional and thought processes, often unconscious and so difficult to navigate. Nevertheless, there are practical steps we can all take to support a shift from a fixed to a growth mindset that in turn can support a shift from trying to manage change to one of change cultivation.

It is generally recognized there are four key steps;

1   from raising awareness (we know self-awareness is a key driver in success and is required for self-acceptance),
2   to giving focused attention to the issue (as this is a highly energy intensive act it will therefore deflect energy from other areas - this can create tension and eventually slippage),
3   performing deliberate and repetitive practice of the new thought or behavior (changing the old saying 'practice makes perfect' to 'practice makes permanent'),
4   and engaging in a purposeful relationship (often with a coach or counsellor) to help keep you on track (remem-

bering it will take a lot of self-management and motivation to keep focused attention and repetitive practice).

Organizational change is really no different, only amplified by the number of individuals involved. As the old Taoist saying goes;

"There is so much to do. There is so little time. We must go slowly."

There is a plethora of research on 'change management' and it would be foolhardy of me to try and replicate it here (see suggested reading list). Nevertheless, a short overview will help summarize the key aspects. King Whitney, Jr, said "Change has a considerable psychological impact on the human mind. To the fearful it is threatening because it means that things may get worse. To the hopeful it is encouraging because things may get better. To the confident it is inspiring because the challenge exists to make things better." Whitney could have been giving a synopsis of DISC personalities:

- **D's** thrive on change and challenge.
- **I's**, the ever optimists, tend to see change as energising.
- **S's** thrive on security and the status quo and fear change if it appears it is for 'change sake.'
- **C's** thrive on rules and regulations, systems and procedures. They do not like taking risks and fear change could be a big mistake.

The more outgoing fast paced personalities 'D and I' are more likely to embrace change if they can see a benefit to their bottom-line or recognition. The more reserved and reflective personalities 'S and C' are more likely to embrace change if they can see the benefit to the team or to the effectiveness of working practices and so a shift towards excellence.

However, due to our 'default' positions, as discussed earlier, we are all likely to focus on different aspects of change and change management. As leaders, it has been argued, it is our responsibility to ensure all aspects of the change management process have been considered for effective implementation, including what are generally termed the 'hard' and 'soft' dimensions; what are often referred to as the seven S's.

The hard dimensions are usually referred to as **strategic, structural** and **systems.** The soft dimensions are usually referred to as the **shared** vision, your **staff** and their **skills** base, and your leadership and management (and so organizational and communication) **style**.

Early engagement of staff in any change process is advised.

As Torrington, Hall and Taylor note "people support what they help to create." Unfortunately, this is a piece of advice that is rarely taken which inevitably results in barriers being erected even before the process has a chance of being implemented and will inevitably lead back to unnecessary conflict. This connects to my earlier point about requiring a shift from an ego driven leadership approach to a more egalitarian position that places people and cultures at the heart of our businesses and society in general.

The issue of 'style of leadership' brings us back to our energizing leader with their key strengths around enthusiasm and optimism, embracing new ideas and spontaneity, networking and collaboration we can see the closeness to what we had earlier termed 'affirmative' leaders. It might be instructive here to think back to the 'emergence' in relation to creativity and innovation. We can see that indeed many of these aspects (connectivity, lack of inhibitors, positive intention and quality of interactions in particular) represent the natural 'default' approach taken by an energising and affirmative leader. Indeed, both affirmative and energizing leaders are on the people side of the DISC quadrant, with affirmative leaders being a bit more patient and steady, while energizing leaders more fast paced and excitable.

My key learning point:

I have more qualifications than I know what to do with. It took me a long time to see this for what it truly was; a false drive for intellect as a way to gain certainty, rather than as a vehicle to creatively and practically benefit others.

We need to accept our fixed mindset to expand our growth mindset.

What is your key learning point?

_____

_____

_____

_____

_____

_____

Chapter Six

F - Fractious Cultures

One of the biggest factors in fear at work is through 'blame' and having a blame culture.

Myles Downey says that to increase performance we need to reduce interference (both self and team interference). By interference Downey means the doubts and fears that act as obstacles to us progressing. As we noted though in the last section 'fear' and so doubts are raised through any change process, whether that be large scale organizational change, individual performance related change, or team working and developmental changes. So we all have fears:

- Someone who has predominantly a D style personality fears failure and the loss of power. If D's find themselves in stressful situations where failure is possible they can become aggressive and blame others as a means to feel in control and stop themselves from feeling weak.

- Someone who has predominantly an I style personality fears the loss of recognition or popularity. If I's find themselves in stressful situations where this loss of popularity is possible they can become frenetic and disorganized and blame others for them loosing face.

- Someone who has predominantly an S style personality fears the loss of security and rapid change. If S's find themselves in stressful situations where there is too much change taking place too quickly they can withdraw or become inflexible and blame others through a passive/aggressive stance.

* Someone who has predominantly a C style personality fears being wrong and failure to achieve expected standards. If C's find themselves in stressful situations where errors happen and standards slip they can become overly critical and insensitive, blaming others for anything and everything less than perfection.

None of these stances is helpful and blame is the biggest barrier individuals, businesses and organizations have to achieving high levels of performance. There is a saying I like, so to paraphrase Wayne W Dyer, author of Power of Intention;

All blame is a waste of time, no matter how much we find fault with others and regardless of how much we blame them it will not change the Situation.

Blame, we know, evokes defensiveness. It is all but impossible to raise awareness and take responsibility when someone feels 'attacked.' Feeling attacked or put upon is when people will invariably revert to fight or flight where our responses become reactive through our perceived lack of choice, rather than proactive which necessitates the freedom to choose. This is often what is referred to as the 'space' between stimulus and response. A fight response will lead to external conflict, while a flight response will lead to internal conflict. Both are likely to exacerbate feelings of anxiety and uncertainty.

Conflict though can be multi-faceted and can come about from anything we attach importance to where there is a level of uncertainty about it.

If something is uncertain and the outcome not guaranteed, we can lose sleep worrying about what is going to happen. This is likely to lead to more anxiety which can result in a perpetual cycle of anxiety, conflict and blame.

ANXIETY = IMPORTANCE x UNCERTAINTY.

How anxious do you currently feel (relate to a specific situation)?

	High	**Medium Anxiety**	**High Anxiety**
Uncertainty	**Low**	**Low – No Anxiety**	**Medium Anxiety**
		Low	**High**
		Importance	

Is this level of anxiety leading to conflict or apportioning blame rather than taking responsibility? If so, what are you going to do about it?

We noted briefly in the Introduction how people with different personality traits can complement and/or come into conflict. Let's elaborate on this potential for conflict.

In the normal run of things D's and C's want to get the task done. I's and S's are more concerned about getting the best out of the people involved. Together this would be a formidable force. However, when different priorities encroach and situations get fraught it can be difficult to reconcile these two elements. Some people can lose sight of the long term goal in the frantic dash to achieve short term targets. While others can place more emphasis on the teams' immediate needs than the long term interests of the business.

Likewise, when things are running smoothly there will be a balance between the fast paced D's and I's, and the more considered pace of S's and C's. In times of change, and especially in the face of external demands, pressure can mount and positions can become polarized. The normal checks and balances, accelerator and brake interplay can be cast aside as the D's and I's steam ahead while the S's and C's become dogged in their resistance and passive/aggression.

Conflict across the DISC styles can erupt during times of intense pressure, such as: D's and S's, with D's being direct and to the point which S's can see as rude and abrasive. S's meanwhile can become overly slow and questioning, which D's can see as lacking urgency, and as negative and defeatist. Or I's and C's due to I's fast paced and frivolous approach which C's can see as lacking in detail and irritating. C's meanwhile, being highly detailed and concerned, can come across as negative and pedantic to I's.

Combined this can all be a heady mix of 'toxic cocktail' that is extremely difficult to get rid of once it has taken root. It has long been recognized that the glue that holds a team together is 'trust.' When conflict is allowed to get out of control trust goes and it is almost impossible to get it back. There are various recognized stages of trust:

1 Suspicious Still, where you don't trust anyone, ever,
2 Suspicious Until, where you only trust someone after they have proven themselves,
3 Trust Until, where you trust people until they let you down,
4 Trust Still, where you trust others even after they have let you down.

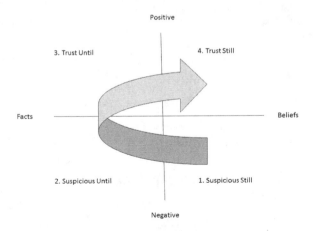

Research has shown that people in positions 3 and 4 (trust until and trust still) tend to be more optimistic and generally more successful due to the recognition that they need to trust their colleagues to perform well and achieve their combined business or organizational goals.

There is a great truism – you must give trust to get trust.

Illustration 1. (a high 'D' senior manager)
   "I don't care about them (staff). I'll drive through what I expect everyone to be working to. That way there is a clear basis from which to progress. They don't like it they can lump it or leave."

Illustration 2. (a high 'I' senior manager)
   "We can all take our feet off the quality brake and get on with generating new ideas and new business. Staff don't need direction; they need freedom to deal with the uncertainties ahead."

The two illustrations above are extremes, and unfortunately only too real. Both are based on a 'default' way of doing things and both led to many casualties.

In the first illustration many good staff were lost, people were riled and unnecessary conflicts ensued. There developed a culture of entrenched passive resistance, especially from staff who thought they no longer mattered as individuals.

In the second illustration too many people lost focus, strategic drift quickly became apparent and underperformance was left unchecked. There was underhanded sniping and an air of chaotic 'anything goes' desperation.

In neither situation was the result that which the leader had desired.

My key learning point:

My life has been littered with blame; my Mum, my Dad, my step-father, colleagues, friends, my partner. My fear of conflict aligned to my fear of trust drove a need for change rather than resolution (it is easier to change the situation that it is to address the issue).

We need to eliminate blame from our thinking in order to enhance our capacity for trust.

What is your key learning point?

_____

_____

_____

_____

_____

Chapter Seven

G - Grow Great Cultures

The question we are left with after the last section is how do we move beyond conflict, or indeed, how do we move beyond any stuck mentality?

There is a short and simple answer to these questions which Confucius supplied in approximately 500 B.C.

"Without learning, the wise become foolish,
by learning, the foolish become wise."

Oh for the simplicity of life. What is this learning we talk of? Who should have it? Why do we need it? How is it accomplished? There are no shortcuts to any place worth going (or to anything worth knowing) and this rings only too true for learning.

The debates around learning, education and training have raged for centuries. Current thinking, to do the dreaded simplification, tend to revolve around four ideological strands:

1 The cultural restorationists who value an elitist culture, national heritage and national curriculum, where teaching is authoritative and for the purpose of ensuring students acquire 'worthwhile knowledge.'

2 The competitive elitists who, like the cultural restorationists, value an elitist culture but with a greater emphasis on future work within society and training the underclass for the purpose of accepting their place in society.

3 The industrial trainers who value the development of habits to do with self-discipline and obedience for the

purpose of work and economic growth.

4   The rational progressives who value reflective practices for the purpose of the development of individuals to reach their full potential.

It is not difficult to see where our current emphasis is placed in the UK when the economy and a single focus on profits dictates too many business and political decisions. But by who? Theorists, politicians, practitioners?

Theory, we are reliably informed, is about the underpinning knowledge of the process of teaching and learning as well as the overall purpose of education within the society we live. Policy at government and institutional levels differ. At government level we are talking about offering a country-wide direction as a means of defining the purpose of education based on the theory and, in theory, backed up by sound research. At institutional level policy defines the rules and regulations staff should be working to so that the institution can achieve its strategic aims and objectives. Practice should be based on an understanding of theory and needs to work within the context of the government and institutions policies and procedures. It is important that practices are refined and developed as a result of reflective practices (research on the ground which then reflects back on theory). So reflection then should be the key to any positive shift: from one theory to another; from one policy to another; from one delivery method to another; indeed, from any position to the next; from moving beyond conflict to growth; or a move beyond any stuck mentality.

The verb to 'reflect' means to think deeply or carefully about something because we want to gain a better understanding of it. Stephen Covey captured this well in his '7 Habits of Highly Effective People' saying 'Seek first to understand, then to be understood.' The verb to reflect comes from the Latin 'reflectere':

to turn back, bend back, turn your thoughts back on something and think deeply about it; to study it, to learn from it, and change or improve what you do next. Reflective practice usually starts from self-reflection and at its best focuses on self-improvement before worrying about improving 'others' or something else.

It is important to develop our self-reflection and wider reflective practices as this will help us in our personal and professional lives, at home and at work. This is part and parcel of the notion of lifelong learning that never stops! It can help us develop our problem solving skills through allowing greater flexibility in our thinking. This in turn will support changes in our attitudes, behavior and so subsequent habits. Otherwise, we are likely to find ourselves in a position where we are walking in circles, getting frustrated when things don't develop our way and don't improve, or when we are not moving forward. As the saying goes, "If you do what you have always done, you will get what you have always got." Or even simpler, as I prefer,

If nothing changes, nothing changes.

The nub of effective reflective practice is sound emotional intelligence (see Daniel Goleman's book 'Emotional Intelligence' and Travis Bradberry's book 'Emotional Intelligence 2' for a great overview, and 'Neuroscience for Leadership Coaching' for the exciting developments this field are giving us to aid our understanding of how our emotions affect thinking and behavior). Emotional intelligence theory was originally developed during the 1970s and 80s by the work and writings of psychologists Howard Gardner, Peter Salovey and 'Jack' Mayer. Although, the earliest roots of emotional intelligence can be traced to Charles Darwin's work on the importance of emotional expression for survival.

Emotional intelligence (usually referred to as EQ, in contrast to IQ) embraces two aspects of intelligence: understanding yourself, your goals, intentions, responses and behavior; and understanding others and their feelings. Emotional intelligence then is aligned to self-reflection and self-awareness and necessitates some kind of change to your thinking or behavior as a consequence of your reflections. As mentioned earlier (see section C) changing habits, i.e. our ways of thinking or behaving, is a difficult thing to do.

Coaching, mentoring or any other 'therapeutic' relationship is recognized as important for keeping us on track and enabling our repetitive new practices to become embedded. Coaching however is not just a set of skills (active listening, questioning, mirroring, paraphrasing, reframing etc, etc) but is rather, like all creative activities, a mindset; a growth mindset we talked about in section E: whether that be for learning and development, to expand your business opportunities, or to support any life, business or creative endeavor that have become 'stuck.' In the coaching context I have found Edward de Bono's Six Thinking Hats useful. De Bono developed a structure for the process of thinking and reflecting, to redirect our thoughts, which entails switching between different aspects, called 'wearing' the appropriate hat. When wearing the;

- Blue hat - you will consider the process involved in the subject you are reflecting on,
- White hat - you will want to consider all the facts objectively,
- Red hat - you will focus on the emotional side of how you feel about the issue,
- Green hat - you will allow yourself to consider creative (and off the wall) solutions,
- Yellow hat - you will think about the potential advantages,
- Black hat - you will consider the potential disadvantages.

This is a great activity when done in the Reality and Options stages of the GROW model which I and many other coaches use. GROW (or more specifically the ToGROW model) is a useful model for ensuring clients move;

- from a generalised topic (To),
- to a specific goal (G),
- the reality (R) of the current situation they are in,
- to the various options (O) open to them,
- and onto what they will (W) do; the specific actions they Will take.

This last stage is the what? when? where? how? and will be SMART (specific, measurable, achievable, realistic and time-bound). I will expand on the GROW Model in section O.

Although the actions at this last stage will be achievable and realistic they will also be stretching and challenging to take the client from their comfort zone into their stretch zone. As it is within our stretch zone we increase our potential and perfor-mance until this becomes our comfort zone (as we discussed in section B). The coaching process then connects changing habits to our ability to become unstuck and move beyond conflict to growth.

Examples of this might be;

- Working with a client who is displaying a high D style personality on issues around 'telling' and micro-managing. These are aspects that can be difficult for high D's in stressful situations when they want things done 'now' and 'their way' – especially if the secondary personality trait is a 'C'. This could take a D/C out of their comfort zone (for those aspects) and place them in their stretch zone, but will enable them to gain engagement and shared responsibility within the team that will better enable them to reach their bottom-line. This will reduce their need to blame others and so reduce the likelihood of continued conflict.

- Working with a client who is displaying a high I style personality on focus and organization to help keep a stressful situation under control. This could take a high I out of their comfort zone (for those aspects) and place them in their stretch zone, but will enable them to gain the recognition they desire from staying on track and following through, which in turn will reduce their need to blame others and so reduce the likelihood of continued conflict.

- Working with a client who is displaying a high S style personality on resistance to change to help them see the business need and longer term benefits. This could take a high S out of their comfort zone (for those aspects) and place them in their stretch zone, but will enable them to gain perspective on why others are taking the approach they are in the current situation that will enable them to better manage their responses. This will allow them to be more flexible and less likely to display a passive/aggressive stance, apportion less blame and so reduce the likelihood of continued conflict.

- Working with a client who is displaying a high C style personality on how perfect perfect needs to be in the current situation and whether good would be good enough. This could take a high C out of their comfort zone (for those aspects) and place them in their stretch zone. This will enable them to be less critical of others input and so reduce their need to blame others performance, and so reduce the likelihood of continued conflict.

While reflection is the prerequisite to becoming unstuck it is not sufficient on its own. We also need an openness to stretch and challenge, to change, and to a clarity of actions that will take us out of our comfort zone and our fixed ideologies. The A to Z Framework and the MIRROR Model offers practical steps in order to change our own thinking, behavior and habits, and ideologies for a deeper level of sustainable change.

Self-reflection

You might like to take some time to consider the following;

- What aspects of your life or work do you currently perceive to be outside your comfort zone?
- How do you intend to address these?
- If there are currently no aspects in your life outside your comfort zone, what aspects could you stretch and challenge yourself on more?

My key learning point:

For too many years the past was a place I did not want to revisit. But without understanding my past how could I live fully in the present? And so I was destined to repeat my change pattern – but from a negative stance rather than from a positive growth position.

We need to develop our self-reflective practices to be able to grow.

What is your key learning point?

_____

_____

_____

_____

Chapter Eight

H - Humane Cultures

Do tenderness, compassion, and sympathy have any place in the business world?

Emma Seppala (2013), and new research in neurosciences, show how minimizing conflict and enhancing compassionate workplaces are good for the corporate bottom-line. How do we do this though and 'keep the edge'?

- First, what do we really mean by terms such as tenderness, compassion and sympathy in the context of the workplace?
- Secondly, how would we measure the direct impact of compassion on the bottom-line?
- And third, what do we mean by 'keep the edge'?

I would suggest that when we talk of tenderness, compassion and sympathy in the workplace we are returning to our discussion around trust and the relationships between people. You would think therefore this would be easier for I's and S's who are both on the people side of the DISC circle, and more difficult for D's and C's who are task orientated. Effective leaders, irrespective of which personality traits dominate, are well aware of how important it is to have people buy-in, motivation and a strongly supportive team ethos. The problem lies in how few truly effective leaders there appear to be.

Let's take a closer look at the personality traits of our leaders from a DISC perspective;

D - Dominant
- D's remember are the Dominant, Decisive, Driver and

Doer. D's like to be in charge. They are direct and want to know 'what' needs done. They will then do it without too much thought; D's can be the proverbial bull in the china shop.

- D's are not naturally great team players and have a tendency to go it alone; going off half-cocked, only to learn the hard way that to get to the bottom-line requires the collective force of the team. A true lesson in humility many D's require.

I - Influencer

- I's remember are the Influencer, Inspirational, Interactive and Interested. I's need recognition and desire to have fun times. They thrive on being in the lime light, and their need for positivity and optimism can put them at odds with the more reserved approach of their fellow S or C team mates.

- I's hate routine and can be very spontaneous. As such they often have to learn to curb their natural 'hot headed' impulsive tendencies to better support the team in their collective endeavours. A true lesson in self-control many I's require.

S - Steadiness

- S's remember are Steady, Sincere, Supportive and Status-Quo orientated. They desire peace, harmony and security. They are consistent, practical and loyal (coming from a place of compassion and love), and are the team player extraordinaire.

- However, S's can also be slow to change, challenge under-performance and take the necessary chances and hard decisions sometimes required of leaders.

C - Conscientious

- C's remember are Conscientious, Competent, Capable, Considered, Critical thinkers. They desire accuracy and logic. They are the great detailed planners who want to work out 'how' things are done.

- Because of their great need for planning and their aversion to risk C's can fall into paralysis by analysis. This accounts for why they often need the direct approach of a D or the impulsive I to get them moving.

There is much to be learnt then from DISCovering who we all are; our leaders and our followers, and how we can all become better team players. This has importance for organizational cultures as we progress from the old command and control style to a more collaborative and dispersed approach where self-awareness and self-management are the order of the day.

That said, we still tend to approach new tasks/ projects/ business opportunities from the perspective of what needs to be achieved; in pursuit of results. If we refer back to Simon Sinek's points about the what, how and why we can see that this approach is very much a 'what.' With this in mind I believe we would be better off starting with the 'why' and then bring in the missing element 'who' (remember our discussion on the change cultivation and the need for early engagement of staff in the hard and soft process).

- Who will be involved?
- Do they have a core understanding and buy-in to the 'why'?
- Do those involved have an understanding of one another?
- Are we clear on each person's individual image of their success and the team's success?
- Do we clearly articulate our hopes, fears, the potential conflict areas and how these can be resolved?

These are all key questions and strategies for establishing and building trust which is so important for the development of high performing teams.

There has been considerable work done around team development stages from the notion of forming, storming, norming to performing, Scott Peck's community driven approach and Stephen Covey's dependences. The key to each of them is that all teams go through stages: from working individually; to conflict and, for more effective teams, bonding and the formation of trust; to a state where 'the whole is greater than the sum of the parts' for highly effective teams that have high-quality relationships, high levels of performance and high levels of success which appear, from the outside, effortless.

Team Development Stages

Forming	Storming	Norming	Performing
Scott Peck updated this to:			
Pseudo community (pretence)	**Chaos** (differences surface)	**Emptiness** (embrace others points of view)	**Community** (space of creativity and insight)
	Fight or flight Differences need to be faced up to in order to move into next stage, or we move back to pretence.	Called 'emptiness' - you have to give up a bit of yourself If we just accept recommendations as a form of deflection, we move back to pretence.	This is where we leave our own agendas aside.

> When conflict does
> arise different
> perspective are
> presented by the
> person with the
> opposing view –
> this flushes out
> misunderstandings.

Stephen Covey matches this to 'characteristics' of the team:

Dependence	Independence	Interdependence
(the energy is turned inwards to the team members)	(the energy is focused on internal competition)	(the energy is directed outwards to common goals)

The goal is not to eliminate conflict. The goal is to shift it from the toxic cocktail that is corrosive to individuals and businesses long term, to the development of passionate disagreement based on a collective buy-in to the core 'why' of the business. A position of passionate disagreement is healthy, creative, non-threatening and energizing. This is a position that allows the business to develop new insights, new approaches, and new avenues for growth. This is what I mean by being able to 'keep the edge.'

Self-reflection

You might want to consider these team development questions;

- At what 'stage' is your team? And what is your evidence for this?
- What actions are you going to take to take your team to brilliance?
- How will you know when you get there? What will it look like and feel like?

My key learning point:

Although I had taken on an affirmative stance (as mentioned earlier) I had also become emotionally distant and aloof, and so really didn't care whether others understood my need for change. This led to a real lack of compassion for anyone who could not 'buy-in.'

We need to clarify our true 'why' so enabling the buy-in of others.

What is your key learning point?

_____

_____

_____

_____

_____

_____

Chapter Nine

I - Inspirational Cultures

"Inspirational leadership is positively correlated with improved individual, group and organizational performance."

Swart, Chisholm and Brown in Neuroscience for Leadership, among many others, believe inspiration comes when we have clarity around our values and higher purpose. Having clarity around our values and higher purpose also gives a sense of freedom associated with our potential.

Freedom though is one of those nebulous terms we all use but rarely take the time to confirm its meaning.

The online Concise Dictionary defines freedom as; "noun; the power or right to act, speak, or think freely." While free is defined as; "adjective; not under the control or in the power of another."

So it would seem freedom is related to 'power to' without being restricted by 'power over.' This relates very much to our discussion on power in the Introduction. In the literature of the social sciences there are various meanings of freedom which come down primarily to; freedom of action and freedom of choice. Freedom of action is when there is nothing or no one who prevents me from doing what I want to do. However, as there are laws and other people to take into consideration freedom in this sense can never be absolute. Freedom of choice is freedom in the metaphysical sense, that is, what causes us to make the choices we do? Do we have free will?

From the point of view of the standard story of action, actions were seen as caused, so the cause of the action must also have been caused by an earlier condition or factor. So either the action could not fail to occur, which is determinism, or you could have chosen otherwise, which is agency. If we accept the story that agents (i.e. you and me – people) cause what their actions cause, but the actions are not the bodily movements - they are something else. What then is that something else? For the philosopher Judith Butler this something else is 'performative re-signification' which is the dialectic of freedom and constraint where possibilities are constituted through discourse (remember we mentioned discourse in relation to memes 'a unit of cultural transmission'). This also connects back to our point in the Fractious section about the 'space' between stimulus and response in relation to taking responsibility and proactive steps that can counter a blame culture.

So what this means is our 'self' is recognizable as repetition and difference, what is called iteration. The philosopher Gilles Deleuze and psychologist Felix Guattari further develop this thinking to find a synthesis of difference and repetition where the 'self' who repeats is composed of a multiplicity of tiny egos, where "habit is the constitutive root of the subject..." This is very much aligned to John Whitmore's notion in *Coaching for Performance* of subpersonalities which is so important to internal conflicts and blockages we come across often in the coaching setting (I elaborate on subpersonalities further in section T). It might be worth referring back to our discussion on changing habits. In this context then freedom could be defined as the power to choose and to act, to change our own thoughts and behavior through challenging our own habits. Very much reflecting Colin Wilson's points about inner freedom, responsibility and an active stance, which combined he calls 'positive existentialism' – a refreshing contrast to the more negative variety of existentialism we are used to encountering (see suggested reading list).

The sociologist T. Bennett notes there is great potential for dissonance due to the "multiplicity of powers that are at play in the everyday." Dissonance, as we know from the fields of leadership and management as well as coaching, happens when we do not live and make choices in line with our values and higher purpose. It is this dissonance that enables us to see the need for positive change (rather than, as previously, mentioned change for change sake). Having clarity around our values and purpose however will not in themselves drive change, or keep people focused, on track and inspired to achieve the desired change. Our values and purpose need to be wrapped around a good story.

Research in the fields of neuroscience and history is beginning to better appreciate what has been common knowledge for millennia: Stories offer insights into the questions 'who am I?' and 'how should we live?' 'Stories' or 'narratives' are important as they give individuals meaning to their lives, affirm our identities, and so validate our values and purpose.

The great (but not always good) guides throughout the history of the human race have been the greatest of story-tellers; Jesus Christ, Muhammad, Mahatma Gandhi, Hitler, Walt Disney, Steve Jobs of Apple and Richard Branson, to name but a few. The power of story-telling has always been understood (consider oral history). Recently though science, and especially neuroscience, has uncovered insights into how our brains mirror some of the activities within stories creating bonds that can lead to changed beliefs, attitudes and behaviors.

We now know that stories are how we make sense of the world. They are how we learn. This is related to what is called 'episodic' memory; the brain's own need for direction and pattern, for cause and effect. Stories fit with our expected pattern; with a beginning, middle and end, and are easily memorable. If stories offer reasons or causes they will be more easily believed as our brains search for meaning, the cause, a purpose.

So we can see why, in a world which is becoming more

complex, ambiguous and uncertain there is even more of a need for inspirational leaders who can tell good stories. This needs to be matched though with high levels of self-mastery - necessary to avoid distortions which the story-tellers themselves end up believing.

My key learning point:

It took a long time for me to comprehend my story, with a key insight coming through my introduction to DISC and understanding that at heart I am an 'I'. And that I was slowly learning how to become the 'I' in the crowd.

We need stories to give meaning to our lives, to affirm our identities, and to validate our values and purpose.

What is your key learning point?

_____

_____

_____

_____

_____

_____

Chapter Ten

J - Judicious Cultures

It is fascinating to think that homo sapiens is derived from the Latin for homo (man) and sapiens (wise) and so defines us as wise men. Especially when we consider it has taken 70,000 years to develop our understanding of our own brains sufficiently to the point where we are only now beginning to really unlock its workings. Our unconscious processes, although still unknown to us, are at last becoming clearer. And our individual personalities which have tantalized us for over two centuries is now becoming knowable. As the great philosopher Immanuel Kant once said,

"If we only knew what we know...we would be astonished at the treasures contained in our knowledge."

The developments that are currently taking place in the study of the human brain and how this relates to the developments in our cultures, organizations and all thinking sapiens out there, at the individual level, will undoubtedly be the driving force behind many of our future stories.

As the world moves into a new phase of technological advancement, scientific understanding and genetic modification, alongside climate change, population growth and resource scarcity, aligned to a hardening of beliefs both religious and secular, we appear to be on a conflict collision course in line with that which took place 60,000 to 70,000 years ago.

Jesus didn't say, "Feed the deserving." He simply said, "Feed the hungry." Yet there are over 1 billion people literally starving to death in the world today. As Mark Shea noted, "The solution is not to kill the child of the poor. It is to demand that our ... corporate system give the poor person what is rightly his:

enough food." As we noted in the last section Jesus was one of the great story-tellers of all time (or one of the greatest characters in one of the greatest stories of all time?)

Who are going to be our new wise men and women that can shape our future stories? Who is going to ensure we do not end up being yet another, as Harari says, "band of storytelling Sapiens (who) were the most important and most destructive force the animal kingdom had ever produced."

We hear a lot about leaders as social agents. But what does this really mean? And why would we do this anyway? Leaders as social agents, if you remember, was how Travis Bradberry defined leadership in the Introduction, and is closely aligned to the notion of leaders as servants of the greater good. But is this how it works in reality? Thwink.org offer a useful visual for better understanding what social agents are and how they work.

How democracy works for its 3 social agents.

In theory | In practice

The People

elect and control

regulates the behaviour of employees/citizens

Provides the jobs, the goods and the services that are the most profitable

The Government

regulates

controls the amount of money and expertise

Corporations

If we accept this image of social agents then we need a better understanding of not just individual personalities and leader-ships styles, but of organizational personality traits and so their expected behavior, especially that of larger corporate organizations.

But how can we tell what an organization's personality traits are?

This is where DISC comes in helpful. We just need to observe and ask a couple of pertinent questions, such as;

- How does the organization present the right way to do things to its staff, customers and partners?
- Is this consistent or does it differ from one part of the organization to another?

The answer to these questions will enable you to gauge which personality trait dominates, or if they change from department to department or situation to situation. This will then allow you to see your place within the organization better, and enable you to find strategies to affect positive change.

So, what might a high **D – Dominant** – organization look like? And what might be effective strategies to enable change for the greater good?

- As with high intensity D individuals you can expect a high intensity D organization to do things the fast way, being decisive in their decision-making. They will be driven by the bottom-line, by being the biggest, most powerful, most profitable. When we think back to our 'quadruple bottom-line model'; profits, people, planet and sustainable progress a D organization will invariably focus on profits to the exclusion of everything else.

- There will be a real air of competitiveness and risk-taking, with lots of would-be bosses fighting for positions of authority. Lots of 'telling' people what to do and expecting it done 'now', with little regard for peoples wellbeing; indeed, there will be a real impatience with those unable to keep up. Failure will not be an option and so there is likely to be a high burn-out rate.

- The notion of looking after the planet for a group of people you don't even know in the long distant future would seem anathema to a high intensity D organization, as with high intensity D individuals with little self-awareness, focused on the now. Goals will be high powered, but short to medium term.

What might a high **I – Influencer** – organization look like? And what might be effective strategies to enable change for the greater good?

- As with a high intensity I individual with little self-awareness or control you can expect an I organization to do things the fun way. This will be a lively, energetic and engaging organization to be in. They will be driven by recognition in whichever field they decide to 'play' in. When we think back to our 'quadruple bottom-line model' an I organization will invariably focus on people to generate enthusiasm to succeed (in whichever guise that is recognized to be).

- There will be a real air of positivity and optimism in this organization. There will be lots of 'selling' and persuading, but with little consideration for those who do not buy-in. There could be a lack of detailed planning and so a number of stalled or unfinished projects which will impact on the organization's profits and sustainability.

- The notion of looking after the planet will be seen as highly laudable to a high I organization, but in an environment of incentives and initiatives, as with high intensity I individuals with little self-awareness, short termism and flirting from one project to another can become the order of the day.

What might a high **S – Steadiness** – organization look like? And what might be effective strategies to enable change for the greater good?

- As with a high intensity S individual with little self-awareness or control you can expect an S organization to do things the traditional and considered way. Steadiness remember will be their buy-line. They will be driven by an appreciation for what they do; the organization doesn't need to be the biggest or most profitable, but it does need to offer security and stability. When we think back to our 'quadruple bottom-line model' an S organization will invariably focus on its people (staff, customers and partners) and will expect and attract brand loyalty.

- There will be a real air of calm wellbeing with lots of listening, consultation, team working and pleasantness. Conflict will rarely be displayed. Change will be slow to embed which can often result in missed opportunities to respond to market demands impacting on the profitability and so sustainability of the organization.

- The notion of looking after the planet to preserve our future will appear to an S organization as the right thing to do. However, their slow and unassuming approach, and discomfort with conflict, as with high intensity S individuals with little self-awareness, can mean they have less impact than they would have desired.

What might a high **C – Conscientious** – organization look like? And what might be effective strategies to enable change for the greater good?

- As with a high intensity C individual with little self-awareness or control you can expect a C organization to do things the right way by following the set rules and regulations. They will be driven by a need for excellence and so being seen as the best in what they do. When we think back to our 'quadruple bottom-line model' a C organization will invariably focus on high end quality and standards that are likely to impact positively on their profits.

- There will be a real air of competence, high levels of performance management, detailed analysis and critical thinking, and detached professionalism in this organization. Lots of 'written procedures' to minimize mistakes and impropriety. However, due to this type of organizations attention to detailed data there can be a lack of acknowledgement of people and their needs beyond the data.

- The notion of looking after the planet to a high C organization would depend on what an analysis of the data tells them. However, their need for accuracy and to make the right decision, as with high intensity C individuals with little self-awareness, can create issues when deliberating on a complex and uncertain future, which can result in paralysis by analysis.

So can we identify strategies to cultivate change within the existing culture?

- First, you can try to change the things or people around you by taking a lead role and enforcing change (this is invariably the route taken in change management attempts).
- Second, you can try and change your own perspective of the situation and so enacting change in yourself (a very therapeutic approach but one that will not necessarily change the actual situation or environment itself).

- Third, you can try engaging in a dialogue that changes all those involved. This is very much a post-modernist/post-structuralist approach where power is productive, change is cultivated through discourse and where 'we' experience a shift in perspective (connected to memes and a shift in culture).

As the philosopher Deleuze and psychologist Guattari state,

"the influence of minds on one another has become an action at a distance." This relates specifically to our capacity for strategic thinking (cultural literacy).

The sociologist Pierre Bourdieu offers three ways to enable this;

- self-reflexive understanding of our own position,
- awareness of the rules, regulations, values and cultural capital that characterise the 'field' (or indeed fields of flow),
- and our ability to manoeuvre within the situation. However, our ability to do this within the complexities of the situations 'we' find ourselves in means we need a greater understanding of those aspects that have been for too long underplayed, that is, the role of biological or genetic factors.

This last point brings us back to the great advancements that are currently being made in the fields of neuroscience, psychology and so leadership and organizational development. It also reiterates a point I made right at the outset of this book; I passionately believe it is my responsibility and your responsibility as leaders and individuals to transform ourselves, to transform our people, to transform the world we live in for the better. It is our combined responsibilities as leaders to become the new wise men and women that can shape our future stories.

My key learning point:

It was through being involved in queer activism in my formative years that I came to understand the need for social agents. This opened up for me a whole new world from which to understand and relate my past, present and future stories.

We need to be the new wise men and women who shape our future stories in order to cultivate the positive and productive cultures we deserve.

What is your key learning point?

_____

_____

_____

_____

_____

_____

Chapter Eleven

K - Killer Cultures

Leadership and management in today's and undoubtedly tomorrow's world revolves around change. Any kind of change, as Charles Darwin noted in 1871, first requires focused attention. Changes however, too often fails to be sustainable, like the aptly named 'coach killer', through being poorly executed. This is primarily due to, on the one hand, focusing on the glory rather than practicing the task itself, and on the other, having too great a focus on the task to the exclusion of the motivational aspects required to keep people on track.

Our change-rich environment has necessitated much more of a cross over between the roles of leaders and managers; of task and people. Put simply D's and C's (task orientated) need I's and S's (people orientated), and I's and S's need D's and C's for any change to occur and be sustainable in a way that minimizes the casualties that change processes have historically left in their wake. And yet nurturing and development is fundamental when talent is the greatest asset companies have.

It has been estimated by the CBI that businesses in the UK spend £39bn annually on formal staff training and development, and that this only accounts for 10% of all training, with the rest being informal and so not recorded or measured. Research by the CIPD shows that training and development has a 22% impact on the bottom-line, and an impressive 88% impact when matched to coaching. Yet questions remain as to how much of this investment is wasted through too great a focus on change management, a lack of sustainable change cultivation and an underdeveloped understanding of the learning process.

As noted previously there are currently exciting developments taking place in the neurosciences that are offering 'road maps' for the future direction of training and development, learning and change at the individual and organizational levels. The correlations between the mind and the organization is having significant impact on a new paradigm for leadership and organizational development. There are clear links with Carol Dweck's 'Growth Mindset', William Marston's behavioral model – DISC – and the new developments in applied neuroscience to business and organizational leadership.

Four key questions all leaders and managers might want to consider are;

1   What work are we doing to raise our own self-awareness?
2   Who do you hold yourself accountable to?
3   Why might it be important to focus your attention on being fully present?
4   How often do you practice new behaviors or attitudes?

The four questions above form the basis of what Swart, Chisholm and Brown call the 'golden circle' in their book *Neuroscience for Leadership*. The process that moves you from consciously trying to think something new to embodied practice; a shift from the old concept of 'practice makes perfect' to 'practice makes permanent.' That is, transformative and sustainable change at the individual and organizational levels.

However, returning to the topic of talent being our greatest asset we might want to ask, to borrow from Bev James in Do It! Or Ditch It! "What behaviors or habits hold you back...?" It might be worth taking some time to reflect on this point.

I have described the main personality traits using DISC as part of Introduction and throughout this book, suffice to say here that irrespective of which personality traits or leadership style you have the lynch pin for all development is the level of recognition you have for its need.

Both leaders and managers need to spend more time getting to grips with their own personality, the personality of the organization, and the energy flow and relationship networks, i.e. the "accumulation of those expensive things called brains that generally walk around on two legs." This is where personality profiling comes of age, and as Swart, Chisholm and Brown further state,

"Our individuality and diversity gives us great strengths. Corporately much of that strength is at risk of being wasted because the management of energy flow in organizations ... is not yet properly understood."

So what do we mean by the energy flow in an organization? It is generally agreed there are four key types of energy flow;

1 Productive energy which is when things are working well and there is a high level of buy-in to the vision, values and purpose of the business or organization, and staff are all working to commonly agreed goals and objectives.
2 Comfortable energy which is when things are ticking along at a steady pace. There will be a feeling of having reached the status quo which could be relaxed fairly laid-back, but has the potential for complacency and lacks stretch and challenge.
3 Resigned energy (or rather lack of energy which would be better described as inertia). Generally, the feeling here is of withdrawal and indifference, and a lack of alignment with any higher set of values or purpose. There is likely to be low performance levels and a reluctance to change.
4 Corrosive energy which is characterised by lack of trust, blame, anger and lots of internal conflict. This is the 'toxic cocktail' we discussed earlier in the Introduction.

Clearly the place any business or organization would wish to be is in the productive energy state. However, this does not just happen and requires continual review and input, and indeed leaders need to understand that all four energy flows could be taking place in various parts of the business at any one time. They also need to be aware of their own impact on creating or fueling any of these energy flows, especially the corrosive which can be a hard lesson to learn.

The trick is to be able to identify the comfortable before it slips into the resigned, and the resigned before it slips into the corrosive. The most obvious ways to do this is to instill new challenges and opportunities that foster shared enthusiasm and effort, but these must be real and not merely manufactured to create a sense of productivity. So connecting back to good and authentic story-telling.

A key issue though in larger organizations is around internal conflict that develop between departments when individuals and teams lose sight of the bigger picture and the overall purpose of the organization and start taking on a them and us mentality. This is a natural part of our evolutionary development going back to tribal systems and behaviors. It is important therefore that people are continually reminded of the larger narrative they are working to. This is where story-telling is highly important for breaking down the inter-departmental squabbles for the sake of a larger 'invented truth.'

Another issue we need to be aware of in our intra-personal, inter-personal and inter-departmental killer cultures that fuel corrosive energy is the natural personality differences that are likely to occur within ourselves, between individuals and between departments that undertake different types of work. DISC does not adhere to the premise that certain personality types are better suited to different roles. DISC rather is about identifying 'how' someone is likely to undertake the role. Nevertheless, research does show that certain personality types do gravitate towards certain roles. The most obvious being high D command and control managers, high I sales, high S customer support and high C finance. But these are very much stereotypes.

DISC however is extremely useful in identifying individual traits and when they might come into conflict, or team traits and which other teams they are likely to come into conflict with. This level of awareness if shared with the teams can lead to a greater understanding of all our default positions, blends, preferred ways of working and communicating, and so how we can all adapt to meet our own and each other's needs. This corrects the misunderstanding 'treat others as **you** want to be treated' to;

'treat others as **they** want to be treated'

Another challenge is to sustain the productive energy flow and this is where the real cross over is now taking place between leaders and managers. Leaders need to have the confidence to support and allow their managers (and staff) to lead which as we have already seen can be all but impossible for old style command and control leaders.

Self-reflection

You might want to take some time to return to and reflect on the four key questions for leaders and managers above.

My key learning point:

My need for change, any kind of change, through the misunderstanding and mismanagement of my own personality, had become a key focus in my personal and professional life. This made it all but impossible for others to keep on track.

We need to recognize that it is our true personality traits that are our greatest assets. These need to be nurtured and developed.

What is your key learning point?

_____

_____

_____

_____

_____

_____

Chapter Twelve

L - Leadership Cultures

"A good leader" say Swart, Chisholm and Brown in *Neuroscience for Leadership* "gets others around him or her to know 'intuitively', how he or she would assign weights to critical issues." This way people in the organization don't just say 'yes', they know what yes looks like and feels like.

So far in this book we have discussed leaders at length, and defined (if loosely) the term leadership, but what is the difference between a leader and a manager? And what are the traits of a good or great leader when they are actually doing their leadership role?

It is generally agreed:

- Managers manage processes; leaders lead people.
- Managers do things right; leaders do the right thing.
- Management is based on a position of power; leadership on earned authority.
- Most organizations have too much management; too little leadership.

There are numerous leadership charts and frameworks. However, some of the most well-known are probably;

- Daniel Goleman's Six Leadership styles,
- Raymond Cattell's Leadership Potential Equation (16 traits in all),
- The Big Five, derived by different researchers but first advanced by Ernest Tupes and Raymond Christal,
- The Eight Dimensions of Leadership put forward by the Inscape Research Team Jeffrey Sugerman, Mark Scullard

and Emma Wilhelm.

Whether we consider Daniel Goleman's Six Leadership Styles, Ken Blanchard's Situational Leadership, or The Eight Dimensions of Leadership which takes a very clear DISC approach we can see there are many correlations between them. What they all have in common is an understanding that no one leadership style is appropriate for all situations and environments. Yet when we match this to the fixed approach to leadership we see in businesses and organizations across all sectors and sizes, and in the wider arena of politics, is it any wonder there is a growing sense of bafflement and concern for all our futures.

What I find fascinating is that each of the frameworks can be clumped into four distinct headings that correlate to the 'rule of four' and the DISC styles Dominant, Influencer, Steadiness and Conscientious, underscored by emotional stability.

Leadership Frameworks

DISC	Goleman	Cattell	Big Five (including emotional stability)	Inscape
Dominant	Commanding	Competitive and assertive when dealing with others, social boldness, tough-skinned, tough-minded-ness, to-the-point, comfortable with criticism	Extraversion	Commanding (Resolute and Pioneering)

Influencer	Visionary	Enthusiasm, (Affiliative) active, expressive, energetic, optimistic, open to change, spontaneous risk-takers	Open to experiences	Energizing (Pioneering & Affirming)
Steadiness	(Affiliative), Democratic, Coaching	They tend to be practical	Agreeableness	Inclusive (Affirming and Humble)
Conscientious	Pacesetting	Sense of duty, compulsiveness, controlled and precise in their social interactions	Conscientious-ness	Deliberate (Humble and Resolute)

If we take our four DISC headings as a starting point, what then does this actually mean good to great leaders do? What might hold some people back from being great leaders? Might having a 'blend' of traits support good leadership? Or would conscious adaptation be more effective than default blends?

D - Dominant Leaders

We have already established a number of traits dominant leaders will display such as taking direct and decisive action that is focused on the bottom-line. They are motivated by a challenge and love to win which gives them great strengths when required to overcome obstacles.

Nevertheless, many of the potential strengths of a D are also the very things that can hold them back from being great, if taken to extreme. There directness can quickly move from bluntness to being down right rude. Their decisiveness can become impulsive and ill-conceived through lack of proper consideration. Their love of challenge can create a tension and corrosion that leads to out and out aggression. And their need to win can undermine a more balanced win-win scenario.

We looked at 'blend' in general during the Introduction. Now let us consider blends specific to D leadership.

For someone with a main D – Dominant trait, the key blends are likely to be with an I – Influencer or a C – Conscientious. Both offer some great additional strengths, such as, adding an extra element of boldness and optimism through a touch of I, giving them real passion and charisma. Or a level of logic and eye for detail through a touch of C, giving them the need to seek out inefficiencies.

I's positivity and optimism however can exacerbate their impulsiveness and lack of attention to detail, alongside a touch of impatience and a need to hog the limelight. While C's methodical trait brings with it an aversion to risk that can stifle their otherwise decisive decision-making and action-taking.

I – Influencer Leaders

We have already established a number of traits influencer leaders will display such as persuading and motivating the team through a positive and optimistic outlook. They are motivated to have fun to gain recognition and love interaction with other people which are great strengths for networking and communication.

Nevertheless, many of the potential strengths of an I are also the very things that can hold them back from being great, if taken to extreme. Their optimistic outlook can become fantasy that lacks any realistic foundation. Their need for fun and spontaneity can lead to a lack of follow through as they switch from one interesting project or initiative to another. Their love of interaction and natural ability to network and communicate can lead to too many meetings and lunches and not enough focus on reaching business goals.

We looked at 'blend' in general during the Introduction. Now let us consider blends specific to I leadership.

For someone with a main I - Influencer trait, the key blends are likely to be with a D – Dominant or an S – Steadiness. Both offer some great additional strengths, such as, adding an extra element of directness and a doer's finisher/ completer approach through a touch of D, giving them real charm and confidence. Or a level of stability and empathy through a touch of S, creating a truly respectful and inclusive environment.

D's directness and doing approach however can lend an arrogance and lack of humility. While S's need for stability and harmony brings with them an aversion to conflict that can mean underperformance is not addressed.

S – Steadiness Leaders

We have already established a number of traits steady leaders will display such as patience, kindness, active listening and consultation, and making people feel valued. They are motivated by acceptance and appreciation and love a sense of peace and harmony which are great strengths for heightened team wellbeing and generating loyalty.

Nevertheless, many of the potential strengths of an S are also the very things that can hold them back from being great, if taken to extreme. Their need for security and harmony can stop them from addressing underperformance in individuals and the organization. Their need for the status quo and doing things the traditional way, and further their steady pace and inclusive approach can make it difficult to harness change quickly enough to respond to new markets, approaches and mindsets needed to be sustainable in today and tomorrow's fast-paced world.

We looked at 'blend' in general during the Introduction. Now let us consider blends specific to S leadership.

For someone with a main S - Steadiness trait, the key blends are likely to be with an I – Influencer or a C – Conscientious. Both offer some great additional strengths, such as, stepping up the pace and bringing an optimism to the organization through a touch of I, giving them a real mixture of people and drive. Or greater planning and a drive for quality through a touch of C, creating a truly excellence driven organization.

I's additional dose of people orientation can lead to a lack of focus on the task and business goals. While C's need for analysis and clearly defined procedures can result in a truly risk adverse organization.

C – Conscientious Leaders

We have already established a number of traits conscientious leaders will display such as careful planning and close attention to quality and accuracy. They are motivated by excellence and doing things right which are great strengths for systematic high quality outcomes.

Nevertheless, many of the potential strengths of a C are also the very things that can hold them back from being great, if taken to extreme. Their need for planning can fall into paralysis by analysis. Their need for excellence can descend into a fanatical drive for perfection. And their love of bring right can generate an arrogance and defensiveness that makes it impossible to see the value of other approaches.

We looked at 'blend' in general during the Introduction. Now let us consider blends specific to C leadership.

For someone with a main C - Conscientious trait, the key blends are likely to be with an S – Steadiness or a D – Dominant. Both offer some great additional strengths, such as, much needed people skills and empathy through a touch of S, creating a friendlier and practically orientated environment. Or a level of pace and decisiveness through a touch of D, giving them an independence and confidence to take calculated risks.

S's need for stability and harmony brings with them an added aversion to conflict that can result in withdrawal when things get tough. While D's forceful and direct approach can lead to an overuse of criticism and sarcasm.

So we can see that all personality traits and blends have potential strengths and potential weaknesses. The point then is not which personality traits or blend of traits are the best set to hold as a leader. The point is how do leaders tap into the required approach that best suits the business or organizational needs at a particular time? This takes us right back to the point I noted in the Introduction, that your response to your environment will determine which of the four traits you display. The choice for leaders then is fairly simple.

Do you:

1 Respond with your normal default trait (or blend)?
2 Or intentionally respond with the trait/s appropriate to the situation, through conscious adaptation?

Being Dominant, Influencer, Steady or Conscientious (or any combined blend) will not guarantee success in itself. What constitutes a great leader is the 'skill' of conscious adaptation, and this is where the 'art' of being a great leader lies. You need to be willing to take an active stance towards your own default traits, with all the attendant psychological and philosophical obstacles that can entail.

My key learning point:

The whole mismanagement of my own personality had meant I had taken on a passive stance towards external impacts.

You need to know yourself before you can hope to actively and purposefully adapt to your environment.

What is your key learning point?

_____

_____

_____

_____

_____

_____

Chapter Thirteen

M - Mindfulness Cultures

Mindfulness is a form of meditation that relates directly to one of the key tools in cultivating sustainable change, i.e. focused attention. Engaging in mindfulness has also been credited with firing creativity and innovation. This highlights the point that the mind was designed to think. The task is not to stop thinking. We are already all too ready to do that (more on that later) but to reach a point of focused attention and relaxed alertness which can aid our great leaders is the 'skill' of conscious adaptation.

"By nature volatile and discordant, the human animal looks to silence for relief from being itself while other creatures enjoy silence as their birthright." John Gray, *The Silence of Animals*

Irrespective of what John Gray says, most human beings seem determined to fill the gaps in those quiet moments at all costs. We tend to feel awkward when things go quiet, so we say something or do something to close down the silence and resurrect noise. Any noise it seems is better than no noise. But this needs to be an external noise which is more a distraction from our own internal noise. For silence does not happen when we stop speaking, or when we go indoors, or when we switch of our TVs, laptops or mobiles. Silence it seems can only happen when we stop thinking.

Our desperate drive for noise then is really a fleeing from our own thoughts. So the search for silence is clearly doomed if we continue to search for it directly, like that elusive search for happiness that can only come about through immersion in something larger than oneself. But because a direct search for silence is doomed does not mean we cannot attain the beauty and power of silence through other means.

1 raising **self-awareness** through self-reflection of our thoughts, emotions and behavior (self-awareness has two key elements, awareness of our thoughts - which is called metacognition - and awareness of our emotions - which is known as meta-mood. Our thoughts and emotions drive our behavior).

2 **acceptance** of who we are and the impossibility of intentionally shutting down our thoughts and emotions. This in itself can be difficult as we have a tendency to live in 'denial' about our true self due, in part, to our socialization process: we are all conditioned through the socialization process which led us to view things in certain ways. To begin to see things in different ways we require some form of (internal or external) intervention, but this intervention needs to have sufficient 'weight' and meaning for it to lead to sustainable change. This process is often referred to as 'deconditioning.' And in part, to our brain functioning and personality traits. Our brains are hard wired in such a way that ensures we are either people or task orientated. This means we will 'naturally' make more use of a network of brain areas connecting the midline (around the dorsal and ventromedial) if we are people orientated, or make more use of the dorsal and ventral attention systems if we are task orientated. What is important to note is that the use of either of these suppresses the other. And within the brain, the strength of either will depend on how often it is used. So if we naturally use one in favour of the other this will become stronger and stronger, while the other becomes weaker and weaker. In order to counter this process, we need to take the time to reconnect with our 'other' side through repetitive use.

3 **focused attention** through repetition (so rather than running away from our thoughts and emotions giving them the attention they deserve). We need to understand that this is a highly energy intensive act that will deflect energy from other areas and activities and so can be difficult to sustain – remember Freud talked about Thanatos in relation to sabotaging our own fulfilment.

4 find our **'inner being'** or as Colin Wilson describes it, taking on a birds-eye view rather than a worms-eye view (this is equivalent to what Maslow notes as self-actualising through taking on the 'flow'). What we referred to above, in relation to happiness, as immersion.

5 **self-detachment** (where self-reflection for self-awareness that leads to self-actualisation and self-realization are only part of a larger journey towards self-transcendence, to paraphrase Viktor E Frankl). Or as John Gray put it "if we turn outside yourself – to the birds and animals and the quickly changing places where they live – you may hear something beyond words. Even humans can find silence, if they can bring themselves to forget the silence they are looking for."

There is a lovely little saying, mindfulness is, "fast becoming the slow way to manage the modern world" which reminds me of the Taoist saying quoted earlier in section E. Mindfulness is becoming aware of and bringing attention to this moment in time. Think back to our 'beginners' mind in Buddhist Cultures which "brings us back to where we can better focus on 'just doing', so when we are eating we just eat, when we are walking we just walk, when we are working we just work and when we are listening we just listen." There are close connections here to what we now understand, through the fields of neuroscience and psychology, as interoception; sustained practice of recognizing and using data that comes from our brain-body axis, our neural system that represents the 'material' or embodied us, sometimes called sense perception. Think about the allegorical portrayals of the five senses! This has significance for self and leadership development as it allows us to have a better understanding of what our bodies are telling us in different situations, such as, raised heartbeat, feeling flushed, tired or energetic and so supports more appropriate decisions and responses based on this knowledge.

We know that in general terms the decision-making process involves the analysis of a finite set of information or data from which we determine alternatives against some (conscious or unconscious) criteria. For years we were led to believe that logical decision-making was the only appropriate option. However, we now know through leadership research, left brain/ right brain findings and through framing theory (I will expand on this in section R), to name but a few, that logical decision-making is extremely limiting, if it exists at all. When there are decisions to be made, especially at times of pressure or in situations of ambiguity and complexity, the so called experts often use their 'intuition', indeed there is growing evidence that suggests complexity making it easier to think 'intuitively' about a situation and thereby make better decisions.

Mindfulness then is a useful tool in the first step towards self-awareness; from self-reflection to self-awareness to self-knowledge that leads to self-mastery in a truly holistic sense.

Key fact: 82% of highly successful business leaders have high levels of self-awareness, only 2% of unsuccessful business leaders have high levels of self-awareness.

Taking these steps will strengthen our leadership skills. It enables us to make better decisions, communicate more clearly and identify our own strengths and weaknesses. This in turn allows us to consciously adapt our approach so it becomes more appropriate to the situation. It also allows us to stop seeking others 'like' ourselves and start to seek out others that complement our strengths and weaknesses thereby building stronger teams within our businesses, organizations and in life in general, where we truly value and embrace diversity.

But let's not kid ourselves, this is by no means an easy process. As John Whitmore noted in *Changing for Performance,* the "journey towards enlightened leadership is far from straightforward, it is challenging, and it takes time." The length of time required will of course be dependent on the changes desired. As noted in *Neuroscience for Leadership* "Things like getting back to the gym can take a few weeks but moving along the spectrum from relying on our logic to taking the chance on our intuition or interoception could be closer to the 10,000 hours of practice popularly quoted to be required for becoming an expert at anything."

Assuming you spend two hours a day every day 10,000 hours would equate to approximately just under 14 years. Is it so surprising then that so few people take this journey? Although I'm sure this is no more time than most of us spend undertaking our leadership apprenticeship before we understand just how little we understand about what it is we have been trying to achieve. Nevertheless, if we recalculate this from the perspective of a normal 8 hour working day we are only talking just over three years. This is little more than the time it would take to gain a Degree or a subsequent PhD, and less than the old strategic planning cycle of three to five years - before we went into annual overdrive.

Being 'asked' to take on the role of Designated Safeguarding Officer alongside my existing role as Inspection Nominee was quite daunting. You have to remember the newspapers had just been full of the Trojan Horse case and the new Common Inspection Framework had been revamped, ratcheting up safeguarding. My heartbeat raced and my nails began to be bitten once more. If we failed because of safeguarding would that be my fault? Would the blame be laid at my feet?

I'm not sure I realized the process I went through at the time, but on reflection it is quite clear. I had raised my own **self-awareness** *through self-reflection on my thoughts, emotions and bodily reactions. It's not pretty having bitten nails. I had then* **accepted** *my own state of fear which projected 'blame' and changed my whole body posture. Especially those wrinkly frowns. This had the result of enabling me to move beyond it to seeing the DSO (Designated Safeguarding Officer) role as meaningful in its own right.*

I then set about **focused attention** *(I did my level 3 Safeguarding for Managers courses again, followed by a level 4 Train the Trainer, for cascading safeguarding training to others, and delved head first into our policies, procedures and case studies) so rather than running away from it, I brought my full attention to it. And to my surprise I did indeed find happiness as immersion (as Colin Wilson put it, finding our* **inner being),** *which in turn allowed me to fall into the flow, transcend my fear, start having fun (even with such a serious subject) and remove that dreaded frown.*

Our Ofsted report used words like 'thorough' and 'proactive', but more importantly our learners were safer and I was an 'I' in its truest positive sense.

My key learning point:

I'm not sure I had ever really paid much attention to my bodily senses, other than my sexual urges. It was a real and growing surprise to me that noticing them enabled me to question my

true motives. They undercut denial and self-deception in a way thinking alone didn't.

We need to better understand and integrate the bodies senses into our decision-making process.

What is your key learning point?

_____

_____

_____

_____

_____

_____

Chapter Fourteen

N - Noble Cultures

As Cardinal Mercier said "We must not only give what we have; we must give what we are." What and who we are is wrapped up in questions of values, beliefs, habits and identities. To truly give of ourselves we need to understand these, often, undefined aspects, which cannot be "prescribed by some outside authority."

If we do want ourselves or our leaders to take the journey to self-mastery we need to be able to identify better our values and beliefs. We touched on these back in the Introduction and it might be worth reminding yourself of the notes you made at the time.

In summary, values are the moral principles a person or person/s hold about what is good or bad, desirable or undesirable. Values have a major influence on how we act, behave and perform so it really is imperative leaders set their own and their business core values explicitly. Beliefs are the things we hold to be true, but which we require no evidence for (invented truths). They are the things which allow us or stop us from doing things. Beliefs therefore are extremely powerful things that support or hinder your own or your businesses success.

The question raised for me here is who are the leaders that are likely to take the time required to become 'great'? But then that would be my question, wouldn't it, being an 'I'. Other questions might be;

- What is the bottom-line here? i.e. what is the benefit of doing all this work for me or my business? How will this give me more authority and a greater sense of freedom? And how can I do this quickly?

- Will all this work be fun? What is the incentive for me or my business? Can it be done with others? Can all this repetition be done in a way that does not become a boring routine?
- Why are we doing it? What will the benefit of this be to me and my team? Could there be a wider benefit to society? How much of this is driven by a need for change, rather than for the sake of change, and will it offer greater security, peace and harmony?
- How do we do this? i.e. what is the actual procedure? Where is the data and information saying there really is a need for all this work? How do we know that after all this work we will get it right? What is the risk involved?

If we can answer each of these questions, then the A to Z Framework and the MIRROR Model will indeed offer real potential for gaining the buy-in of all our 'potential' great leaders irrespective of which default personality trait/s they display.

So let us try and answer these questions now.

- Some possible D Questions

Q. What is the bottom-line here? i.e. what is the benefit of doing all this work for me or my business?
A. The point of self-mastery is more control over our own destiny and the success of our business. Research shows us that 82% of the most successful leaders have high levels of self-awareness, while only 2% of leaders who have not been successful have high levels of self-awareness.

What are your thoughts?

Q. How will this give me more authority and a greater sense of freedom?

A. Being in control of your own destiny by definition gives a greater sense of freedom to reframe your success, open up new opportunities and re-energize you to capitalize on these opportunities.

What are your thoughts?

Q. And how can I do this quickly?
A. By immersion. We know that the more you immerse yourself, give focused attention to any subject, the quicker you will master it.

What are your thoughts?

- Some possible I Questions

Q. Will all this work be fun?
A. By becoming a master or expert on anything allows for a certain lightness and fun that often escapes those less confident in the subject.

What are your thoughts?

Q. What is the incentive for me or my business?
A. The incentives are that self-mastery enables improved communication, enhanced motivational skills and so greater recognition and influence.

What are your thoughts?

Q. Can it be done with others?
A. Self-mastery to a great extent is a personal journey, although doing it with the aid of a 'powerful relationship' is advised as only then can 'we' progress.

What are your thoughts?

Q. Can all this repetition be done in a way that does not become a boring routine?
A. Most of life is lived through 'repetitive practice.' It is our choice whether that becomes boring routine or positive iteration which leads to peak experience.

What are your thoughts?

- Some possible S Questions

Q. Why are we doing it?
A. To change our thinking and doing practices, to enable better communication and so reduce conflict and ensure more harmonious environment.

What are your thoughts?

Q. What will the benefit of this be to me and my team?
A. Teams will be much more trusting, more sensitive to each other's needs and so more loyal to each other and the company.

What are your thoughts?

Q. Could there be a wider benefit to society?
A. If we transform ourselves and our team/s, then we begin to transform the world we live in for the better.

What are your thoughts?

Q. How much of this is driven by a need for change, rather than for the sake of change, and will it offer greater security, peace and harmony?

A. Greater self-mastery brings with it the ability to connect more effectively with others. This is indeed change that is greatly needed in today's world of negativity and conflict, to ensure greater harmony and security.

What are your thoughts?

- Some possible C Questions

Q. How do we do this? i.e. what is the actual procedure?
A. Throughout this book there are various activities to support self-mastery. Towards the end of the book we move onto the 'Pulling it all together' section which goes into detail on the A to Z Framework and the MIRROR Model and its practical steps.

What are your thoughts?

Q. Where is the data and information saying there really is a need for all this work?
A. See the recommended reading list that will show how vital this work is.

What are your thoughts?

Q. How do we know that after all this work we will get it right?
A. There are no guarantees with the future. What we do know is that without the minds of great critical thinkers with high levels of self-mastery we can't even begin to plan for a better future.

What are your thoughts?

Q. What is the risk involved?
A. The greatest risk we face is our own fears; of failure, of the loss of recognition, of the loss of security, and of not getting it right.

This too often drives us into a state of comfortable self-deception and denial.

What are your thoughts?

History shows us the great strides we have taken and the power we now have to remake or obliterate the world we live in for good. As we move into the next stage of human evolution, intelligent design and organizational development it is imperative we have the leaders who are capable of self-reflection, self-awareness, self-knowledge and self-mastery to counter the 'irresponsible gods' we could otherwise become.

If we refer back to our earlier point about beliefs being the things we hold to be true but which we require no evidence for (invented truths) this leads us nicely on to an understanding of the need for a pragmatic stance where the focus is not on the truthfulness of our beliefs but rather the consequences of holding them.

My key learning point:

For years now my intellectual posturing had been falling on my own deaf ears. And I began to see this was due to a romantic affiliation with my own ivory tower right brain. But with no connection to a left brain pragmatic model that could bring both aspects together for effective implementation.

We need to take a leap of faith to become our own future story-telling wise men and women.

What is your key learning point?

Chapter Fifteen

O - OOPS Cultures

In *Co-Active Coaching* the authors playfully talk about OOPS; over optimistic planning syndrome. This is where our motivational fire has not been tempered by the realities of the environment we find ourselves in. In order to achieve success with our goals, our actions must be stretching, challenging and so by definition optimistic, yet realistic in their optimism. The goal therefore is not to change the world as we know it, but rather to transform those aspects that are within our control; so transform ourselves, 'our' world and 'our' businesses.

There are many different models for planning to ensure we don't fall into OOPS. In the business world most people will have heard of SWOT and PEST. In the coaching world there is the Co-Active model, the Thinking Environment and many more. One of the best known models in the cross over between the coaching and business worlds and the one I often use; the GROW model. The GROW model was developed out of various sources but owes much to the thinking of John Whitmore. Whitmore places GROW within the context of self-awareness and responsibility. Without either self-awareness or taking responsibility the GROW model (and indeed any model) will be redundant. However, as we progress our self-awareness and self-mastery we increase our sense of responsibility, ownership, belief and performance.

Combining SWOT and PEST with ToGROW offers a hybrid model that covers many bases. Let's have a look at them.

The ToGROW model starts by understanding and defining the 'Topic' or subject area to be considered. During any planning process the topic stage could be broad and generic to start with and might need to be condensed and brought into focus around the specific aspect to be worked on. Or might be highly focused and specific and need to be further expanded and developed to ensure the focus is appropriate to the big picture.

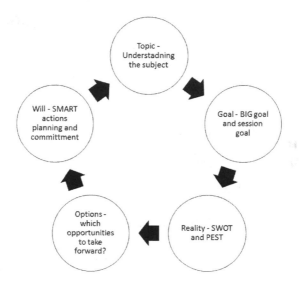

Topic

It is important at this initial stage to clarify which aspects are the important ones to be worked on right now otherwise you can end up setting goals and planning for things that are not your immediate priorities. This can be a difficult stage for some of our personality types.

- Those with a high D - Dominant trait could find this stage irritating as they are likely to already 'know' what they want to focus on, the kind of goal they want to set and the actions to be taken. Job done. It is important D's are challenged to consider the wider field, where their assumptions driving their decisions have come from and other strands (especially in the detail) that may have been overlooked. They will also need to be supported to look at the consequences of doing and not doing what they are focused on, especially in terms of success and failure.

- Those with a high I - Influencer trait could find this stage equally challenging as they are likely to have lots and lots of different ideas they want to focus on or incorporate. They will need to be challenged to hone down the field, focus on the detail and better define the topic. They will also need to be supported to look at the consequences of doing and not doing what they are focused on, especially in terms of recognition or loss of popularity.

- Those with a high S - Steadiness trait could find this stage challenging for different reasons. As they are likely to want to keep the status quo and take a slower pace than time permits they might need to be challenged about these aspects. They will also need to be supported to look at the consequences of doing and not doing what they are focused on, especially in terms of the harmony or temporary loss of security it could create.

- Those with a high C - Conscientious trait could initially find this stage an irrelevance. They are likely to have already done all the research and fact finding and 'know' what they want to focus on in detail. However, having delved so far into the detail they are likely to have missed the big picture. It is important they are challenged to take the time to do so. They will also need to be supported to look at the consequences of doing and not doing what they are focused on, especially in terms of perfection and potential risks.

Goal

Initially the goal is likely to be fairly broad based. It has often been questioned why, using the GROW model, goals are set before the reality of the situation is established. The rationale for this is that research shows us that goals set before a reality check tend to be more aspirational, yet achieved, while those set after a reality check tend to be less aspirational. A reality check tends to draw out the negatives which reduce our levels of confidence in our abilities to achieve stretching and challenging goals.

The goal stage will have its own difficulties for our personality types.

- Our D types, as previously mentioned, will probably have come with the goal in mind, but might need to be challenged to confirm it is the right goal. They will also need to be challenged on how realistic the goal is in the timescale, or with the resources or support mechanisms available. They might need to be encouraged to break the goal down into chunks to better 'sell' it to the team otherwise the team could be thrown into a state of panic.

- Our I types will probably come at this stage with big ideas, big goals and lots of them, but might need to be challenged to confirm which is the most important at this time and the magnitude of it. Like the D's our I's might need to be encouraged to break the goal down into chunks to offer a stepping stone approach to ensure they are achievable.

- Our S types will probably come at this stage with fairly easy and comfortable goals to achieve. They might need to be challenged to step out of their comfort zone and supported to move into their stretch zone in order that the goal has sufficiently meaningful impact.

- Our C types will probably come at this stage with a prepared goal or set of goals tending towards the perfectionist extreme. They will need to be challenged first to ensure they have sufficiently taken into account the big picture (and the people picture). Secondly they will need to be supported to question how realistic perfectionism is and what level of precision is actually required in the current situation, and so whether the goal is aspirational or just unachievable.

Reality

The reality stage of any planning process is where we need to draw out our wider knowledge of the current situation; the strengths and weaknesses, and any obstacles or barriers, the detail and the big picture. As mentioned earlier useful tools for doing this are the SWOT and PEST analysis.

SWOT stands for strengths, weaknesses, opportunities and threats. These can be used from an organizational, team or individual perspective. SWOT is usually displayed as four segments of a square;

Strengths
What makes you, your team or your organization stand out? What are you really good at?

Weaknesses
What are you, your team or organization not so good at? What are you struggling with?

Opportunities
Are there new opportunities to be taken advantage of? Things that can help address what you are not so good at or struggling with?

Threats
Are there things coming up on the horizon that could challenge you further? Limit you further? Limit your growth or potential?

PEST stands for political, economic, social and technological. These are great for seeing your business within a larger landscape or context.

Political
Government drivers or policy shifts that could impact on your business.

Economic
Current economic conditions and future forecasts that could impact on your businesses sustainability.

Social
Trends or changing demographics that can impact on society, culture, work and so impact on your business.

Technological
Developments in new technology for new marketing opportunities, competition, online safety and sustainability.

It would be useful in an organizational or team environment to do this from the different DISC styles, or using Bev James DISC Walk at an individual level, to gain insight from all perspectives that can then be brought together to give a real depth of consideration.

As with the Topic and Grow stages, the Reality stage can cause some difficulties for our personality types.

- For our D's who have already decided on the topic and goal - having swept over the landscape - this stage can seem a waste of time, and indeed can appear to hold them back from getting on with the task at hand. These Doers will need to be challenged to consider broader aspects or can end up going off half-cocked.

- For our I's this stage can appear overly negative and so something that needs to be dealt with a quickly as possible, but as they can suffer from OOPS they will need to be challenged to focus on the potential obstacles and challenges. This is a good stage in which to focus I's on the consequences of not achieving the stated goals.

- As mentioned above, research shows us that the reality check stage tends to draw out the negatives which reduces our levels of confidence in our abilities to achieve stretching and challenging goals. This can have disastrous effects on our S's who by nature want to play it safe. When in this stage S's need to be challenged to recognize the positives and the successes.

- For a C this stage can descend into an overly detailed analysis of everything that has gone wrong before. As with the goal stage they will need to be challenged to consider how perfect perfect needs to be, and how people are being affected and communicated to enable empowerment and buy-in.

Options

The Options stage of the planning process is often referred to as the creative stage. This is where ideas are generated, no matter how off the wall. It is a well-researched phenomenon that off the wall ideas are invariably ditched. But it is opening ourselves up to these ideas that lead to a fertile field from which the 'good' idea you end up running with comes from. To close ourselves off from this stage is to stifle creativity, innovation and our entrepreneurial spirit. Nevertheless, this stage also caused some challenges for our personality types.

- For D's who have had to endure a slog through the Reality stage they will want to move straight onto the Will stage as soon as they have an Option to their liking. They will need to be challenged to keep the creative process open.

- I's will in general find this stage a fun place to be. They are likely to unearth lots of Options. The challenge will be to keep them on track so the options are related to the initial goal set.

- S's are likely to fall back into playing it safe if not challenged to embrace this creative Options stage. They will need to be challenged to remember that these are only options and supported to look beyond their comfort zone.

- C's tend to filter their own thought process so they don't appear 'wrong.' This is a great inhibitor and C's need to be supported to verbalise their thoughts at this stage in a safe environment that allows them to see new potentialities. For a C this cannot be a quick stage.

Will

The Will stage is the Way Forward. The action planning that will be SMART. SMART as an acronym has been variously described and relate to **what**, by **whom, how,** and by **when.** The letters usually stand for;

- Specific
- Measurable or meaningful
- Achievable or action orientated
- Realistic or relevant
- Timely or time-bound

Like each of the other stages, this stage has some specific challenges we need to consider.

- For D's this is a good stage. D's like taking action. The key point to look out for here is that the actions have realistic timeframes based on the information gleaned from the Reality stage.

- For I's setting actions is not an issue so long as they see the fun attached to the actions. The issue is likely to be the follow through if there are too many actions, or if motivation is lost due to losing sight of the 'why' and the purpose behind the action.

- For S's action planning is no great difficulty so long as the plan allows them to approach things at the desired pace. They are completers and will want to know that the actions are having a beneficial impact on the team as a whole.

- C's tend to gravitate to this stage. They love planning, but can become so embroiled in the detail they can spend so long on the plan they forget to actually take the action. C's will need to be supported to consider how everyone who needs to be is communicated with appropriately on how the plan will impact on them.

For the pragmatic this process offers a stepping stone into reframing (which we will discuss in section R) that allows us to take responsibility once more, but from a more creative position that will enable us to take the leap required for change to occur. Change (transformation) of the self before any other transformation can truly be of value.

My key learning point:

My own OOPs and UOPs (over and under optimistic planning) had led to a growing cynicism that allowed me to justify holding others responsible and giving up my own ownership of the impact I have on my own life and on others.

We need to cultivate a sense of responsibility, ownership and belief that allows for a transformational leap.

What is your key learning point?

_____

_____

_____

_____

_____

_____

Chapter Sixteen

P - Purposeful Cultures

Sound planning reinforces a purposeful culture that enables us to better focus on our quadruple bottom-line. Irrespective of which DISC traits you have and the difficulties inherent in different stages of the planning process for each of us our motivational fire will be buoyed up by knowing we have a sound plan behind us. More than this, the planning process allows us to connect with and articulate once more our 'purpose.' As George Bernard Shaw said "...the true joy of life, the being used for a purpose recognized by yourself as a mighty one...the being a force of Nature instead of a feverish selfish little clod..."

We discussed 'purpose' as part of our Introduction section (the core 'why' of your business), and in section K we looked at energy flows, where 'productive energy' was seen to be when things are working well and there is a high level of buy-in to the vision, values and 'purpose' of the business or organization, and staff are all working to commonly agreed goals and objectives. Purposeful cultures therefore need to be highly people focused, and help and empower people to think for themselves. This sounds fairly straightforward. However, identifying your own purpose or the purpose you bring to the business is no easy matter. Indeed, if this is not identified dissonance can occur which in turn can lead to interference as we noted in section F. But how do we start going about identifying our own 'why'?

We could start by questioning our core drivers in terms of our desires, needs and motivations. Desire is a sense of longing, where the thought of gaining what we desire excites us enough to take action to ensure we get what we desire. Need is where something is essential or necessary, as opposed to desirable. Need therefore does not have the strength of emotional attachment desire does, but can vary in compulsion from our 'basic' need for air, water and food to live to our need for self-esteem or self-actualization (consider Maslow's hierarchy). Motivation is the reason we take action or behave in particular ways.

There are lots of different theories surrounding motivation, with the most widely known being;

- The Intrinsic/Extrinsic Model. Intrinsic motivation is something specific to the individual while extrinsic motivation is something that comes from outside of the individual and acts upon them (connected to the old 'carrot and stick' approach of rewards and punishment). It has long been recognized that intrinsic motivators are more sustainable while extrinsic motivators will be dropped once the initial carrot or stick has been applied. For years competition was seen as a great external motivator, however, we now realize this only works for some personality styles and not others.

- The Push/Pull Model. Push motivation is where individuals take action directed specifically towards their goal. Pull motivation is where the individual *desires* the goal so much they feel they are being pulled towards it. Pull then is much stronger motivator than Push. As Push is more difficult, although usually seen as more beneficial and positive goals, this entails a much higher level of self-awareness, self-control and self-management (think back to our discussion around mindfulness and the leadership journey in sections L and M).

- One of the most recent models is Games Theory. Games Theory is "the study of mathematical models of conflict and cooperation between intelligent rational decision-makers", according to Roger Myerson in his book *Game Theory: Analysis of Conflict*. The notion of 'games' is connected to the sociologist Pierre Bourdieu's theories around 'field', where we need to know the rules of the game to be effective; links therefore between 'field' and 'habitus' that limit our capacities. Even when expanded through the philosopher Gilles Deleuze and the psychologist Felix Guattari's systems of fields of flow where "the influence of minds on one another has become an action at a distance" there would still be limitations. Motivation therefore becomes central, as without motivation a player in the game will not be interested in progressing further. This has clear implication for the business world and the need for staff and customer engagement with our business goals, as this drives how motivated they are (or not) to take the desired action.

It is interesting that Jon Radoff, an American entrepreneur and games designer, has put forward a four-quadrant model of 'gameplay' motivation (achievement, competition, cooperation and immersion) which on the face of it looks remarkably like the motivations, desires and preferences of our four DISC personality types. Success in achieving the bottom-line is the key desire of a D – Dominant style. Incentives and friendly competition is the preferred way of working for an I – Influencer style. The preferred way of working for an S – Steadiness style is through cooperation. Immersion, as a way to ensure the expertise required to know you are right, is a key approach of a C-Conscientious style.

It was insightful when doing my research for this book just how little understanding there was evidenced around staff motivation; some leaders and managers said specifically they paid no interest to staff motivation; others said they thought it important but they themselves did not understanding what their staff's motivation might be; others took a very 'C' systems approach or a 'D' decision-making approach and one related this specifically to her own 'I' need for praise and recognition, therefore assuming others had the same motivational drivers.

Let's look at the motivational drivers of our DISC personality styles and question how we, as leaders, can galvanize our staff through tapping into these motivations.

D – Dominant style motivations

- D's are motivated by control and challenge so they can have success and power. In a practical sense at work this means our D's want to be in control of their own work environment and the task/ project in hand. These are the people who will search out a challenge, address ineffi-ciencies, and drive things forward using as direct a means as possible to reach the bottom-line.

- For leaders what this means is ensuring D's are given new opportunities and new challenges which offer the potential for advancement through success. It also means taking a much more hands-off approach to supervision so they feel much more in control of their own working ways and environment. This hands-off approach can be difficult if you are a C – Conscientious style leader who wants to know the detail, or indeed, another D who wants to make all the decisions.

I - Influencer style motivations

- I's are motivated by having recognition and fun through interactions with other people. In a practical sense at work this means our I's want lots of engagement, acknowl-edgement, positivity and friendly competition to support spontaneity. These are the people who will drive up the enthusiasm of the team, ensuring the generation of new ideas and creative solutions that can drive the business towards achieving its bottom-line.

- For leaders what this means is ensuring I's are given lots of opportunities for interaction with others, lots of praise and recognition for achievements, and are encouraged to seek out new ideas and solutions. This more upbeat, fast paced, informal and friendly approach can be difficult if you are an S – Steadiness style leader who appreciates a slower pace with little change, or a C – Conscientious style leader who wants a more methodical, professional (stand-offish) approach.

S - Steadiness style motivations

- S's are motivated by appreciation and acceptance so they can have peace and harmony in the work place. In a practical sense this means our S's want a consistent, steady and reflective environment where people cooperate, are thanked and consulted in the decision-making processes that affect the security of themselves, others or the business. These are the people who will be looking out for the wellbeing of the team, ensuring we are all in a 'good' place to be able to achieve the businesses bottom-line.

- For leaders what this means is ensuring S's are given lots of opportunities to work collaboratively and consistently, with lots of reflection time and explicit support from the leadership team. It also means when change is required S's need to be as fully engaged as possible, offering a clear rationale of the need for the change. This more paced and considered approach can be difficult if you are a D – Dominant style leader who thrives on change and directness, or an I – Influencer style leader who desires fast paced fun, or a C – Conscientious style leader who is more comfortable with facts and data than the feelings and emotions an S can display.

C - Conscientious style motivations

- C's are motivated by excellence where things are done the proper and right way. In a practical sense at work this means our C's want a logical, systems driven approach that clearly leads to quality and accuracy. These are the people who will have a focus on the detail, the data and the facts ensuring there is a clear and precise plan in place to enable the business to achieve its bottom-line.

- For leaders what this means is ensuring C's are given opportunities to display their expertise, ensure clarity of instruction, explanation and direction, and make sure C's have opportunities to feed into long term systems driven quality processes. This methodical and precise approach can be difficult if you are a D – Dominant style leader who likes to do things the fast way with lots of change, or an I – Influencer style leader who doesn't do detail or (perceived) negativity, or even an S – Steadiness style leader who dislikes insensitivity and coldness.

We can really get a sense here of why it might be that motivating others to buy-in to a purposeful business or organization is no easy task. There needs to be an alignment between your leadership style, the individual's personality style, the organizational style and an openness to engaging in a developmental process that challenges and supports us all to raise all our individual levels of self-awareness. And this runs counter to our existing cultural norm.

Although the responses I noted above to staff motivation was insightful, the responses I received specific to customer motivations was really quite frightening. Responses ranged from 'not sure' to 'I suppose we should know their needs.' There was a real lack of clarity and a vagueness throughout. In one instance the response was 'we do understand, but we don't cater for them.' Many responses related customer motivations to systems and finances, and in one instance the response was 'meeting my own needs is more important.' This really emphasizes the potential mismanagement, denial or self-deception we spend much of our lives in and so the breadth of missed opportunities around cultivating the motivation of ourselves and others to reaching our own, collective or businesses true potential.

Self-reflection

You might like to take some time to consider the following questions;

- Are your own motivational needs being met? If not, how are you going to address this?
- How are you proactively eliminating the de-motivational factors that currently exist in your life or work environment?
- How are you offering sufficient motivational opportunities for each of your team to buy-in to the goals of the business? If you are not currently doing so, how are you going to address this?
- How does your employee engagement and developmental process encourage self-awareness in yourself and your staff?

My key learning point:

Although for years I would have said my motivation was to consider an alternative and better way of existing. The reality

was quite different. I was actually motivated to keep myself safe through distancing myself through a lack of engagement.

We need to pay attention to what 'truly' motivates ourselves and others. This is the most effective way to secure real success.

What is your key learning point?

_____

_____

_____

_____

_____

_____

Chapter Seventeen

Q - Queer Cultures

We are highly driven by leadership cultures that have come out of the command and control approach. However, with the rise in social networks and a belief in empowerment and egalitarianism this approach is no longer appropriate or effective. And indeed is counter to the needs of our 'complex dynamic system' with high levels of uncertainty and ambiguity. In our current and future business world real control for leaders and followers alike will come through self-awareness and self-management.

Our future culture/s need to be shared ones, based on motivational factors of trust and respect, underlined by congruent value and belief systems. This is counter to our existing dominant approach, but is a trajectory everyone who believes they are 'responsible' for and deserve input into 'owning' their culture can influence.

If I am right on my assertion that most organizations are still in 'command and control' then coaching, which is about helping others think for themselves, must indeed be a very queer practice. But a practice that is sorely needed if we are to take ourselves and our businesses towards the next evolutionary jump to fully and purposefully engage with the shifts taking place in the wider arena. When considering our own businesses, the culture is likely to be set through a combination of our own 'default' personality traits, our leadership style, our staff's personality traits, our followers behavior, and the inter-relationship between these various aspects. There is a well knows saying 'always a leader, never a follower be' which sorely misunderstands the relationship between leader/ follower and the role followers play in enabling or crippling success.

So, what do we mean by this term 'followers'? And am I being condescending here? The word follower does have negative connotations. Conjuring up images of passivity, drift and submission. A common portrayal of what the philosopher Judith Butler calls 'passionate attachment' to our oppressors. Butler talked about our 'passionate attachment' to the power that dominates us, from the first example of child to parent, where our very survival depends on those in power. So we need to justify ourselves as we already recognize 'authority of the law', such as women's need to prove themselves to men, gays and lesbians to heterosexuals, blacks to whites, the worker to the boss, the uncultured to the cultured. This is highly reflective of our beliefs which "have the power to create or destroy" as The Coaching Academy highlights. These beliefs can hold us back and need to be challenged if we are to unlock our own and our businesses potential. This highlights the need for leaders to have posed to themselves the question "how aware are you of the belief systems that are driving you?" and further to share this thinking with their followers.

In fact, being a follower (coming out of Follower Theory, an off-shoot of Leadership Theory) is a very active stance and a position we all 'take' at different times and in different situations. Being a follower then is not a role assigned to you, but a behavior we enact at a particular time in relation to the leader at that time. So leader and follower is a co-constructed relationship. A relationship that nevertheless is heavily dependent on the communication strategy taken by the leader for its success or failure. It is through the appropriate communication strategy that a leader can facilitate followers support for any change process; to influence follower's commitment requires participation otherwise we are setting up a likely scenario for resistance.

So it is through the effective use of communication strategies that we generate good working relationships, get buy-in to change and enhance the chances of everyone working to secure success for our business goals through synthesis. In leadership theory it is generally accepted that 'power distance' leads to poor communication, poor team ethos and high levels of uncertainty; the necessary ingredients for conflict, blame and cultural toxic cocktail. Communication then needs to have an up close and personal element. Indeed, if we think back to our discussion on 'memes' as transmitters of culture some would say;

Culture is communication, communication is culture.

There is a generally held assumption that communication with staff is about telling, selling, participating and delegating. Which approach is dependent on the competence, confidence and engagement level of those involved. When staff have a low level of competence and confidence, so the story goes, we tell them what to do. When they are confident and engaged, we sell to them which in turn ups their motivation levels. When they are capable but have low levels of confidence we facilitate participation which boosts their confidence and engagement, so we can then sell to them and so enhance their motivation. When they are capable, confident, engaged and motivated we delegate. This more or less correlates with Ken Blanchard's Situational Leadership Model.

However, even though this general approach is still widely used, it is dated in light of the changing nature of organizations which have become much more organic, with employee expectations around cooperation and self-organization, and interconnections and networks at the micro and macro levels. Communication in this context needs therefore to be reframed around both the individual and the organization. From an organizational perspective we need to understand the culture in order that we adopt the appropriate approach generically when communicating to groups. From an individual perspective we need to understand individual cultures (i.e. their personality) to ensure more effective and meaningful exchanges that convey the intended message, very much in line with Stephen Covey, 'Seek first to understand, then to be understood' in *The 7 Habits of Highly Effective People*. This is a process, he says, that you cannot rush;

"slow is fast; fast is slow"

For Covey this is the foundations of communication, and is based on sincerity and the realization that you cannot be efficient with people.

I'm sure you will have heard the saying 'I say what I mean and I mean what I say.' This we now know to be rarely, if ever, true. There is invariably a gulf between what people say and what they mean. If only communication was that simplistic, we wouldn't spend our lives in a perpetual state of conflict and misunderstanding. Take the simple phrase 'that wasn't what I wanted.' You couldn't be clearer. Could you?

Well let's consider that. If I say 'that wasn't what I wanted', what I really mean is, 'I wanted something else.' Possibly something I'm certain I'd explained quite clearly to you, or potentially something I hadn't explained at all but assumed you would know.

But the message you might have heard is;

- 'Let's fight about this because you are challenging my power base.'
- Or possibly 'I don't like you anymore.'
- Or what about 'I don't appreciate what you have done and all the extra work you put in.'
- But it could just as easily have been 'you've done this all wrong, you're incompetent.'

But as we all know communication is second nature to us all.

After all, don't we communicate every minute of every day?

Communication though is not nearly as easy as we let ourselves believe. Although what I really mean by 'communication is not nearly as easy as we let ourselves believe' is;

- you are really pretty crap at it,
- or I have a negative streak and I'm taking the fun out of it,
- or I'm a bully and expect you to do things my way,
- or quite possibly the system you thought you worked to doesn't work, and of course, it's your fault.

So, how do we speak a common tongue that can be more easily understood by all (or at least most)?

When Dr. William Marston published his book *The Emotions of Normal People* he wanted to know how we can better understand each other in normal situations. Marston believed that if you know your own and other's 'default' traits you will be in a position to communicate more effectively, cut off potential conflict situations at the pass, and influence your own or your team's potential for success.

So how does this help when communicating?

If you know someone's default trait is Dominant, Influencer, Steadiness or Conscientious you can adapt your default communication style.

- Dominant styles want to 'tell' it as it is.
- Influencer styles want to 'sell' it through persuasion, positivity and fun.
- Steadiness styles want to 'listen and consult.'
- Conscientious styles want it 'written down' with lots of attention to detail and clearly defined explanations.

Communication has no quick fix, but does have **predictable** approaches that can minimize confusion and conflict, and ensure we get across as near to the message we are trying to convey as is possible. So let's take a closer look at what DISC shows us about communicating with each of the DISC personality styles.

D – Dominant and communication

- When communicating with a D be direct, no waffle, be brief and keep it solutions orientated. For some high intensity D's this can mean no small talk, cut the friend-liness, get to the bottom-line. However, when being this direct there can be a deficit of detail so you might need to follow up your initial communication with a detailed report – so long as it contains an easy referencing system or it will languish unread.

- You will need to show confidence and self-assurance, as well as tact and respect for their competence base when communicating with a D. Even when Ds are capable, confident and engaged don't 'sell' to them. D's hate being sold to as they will think they are being taken advantage of in some way.

I - Influencer and communication

- When communicating with an I keep it light and upbeat to feed into their positivity. Unlike a D, I's are happy to talk and talk and expect friendliness, openness and lots of informality. However, when being this fluid there can be a lack of focus so you might need to clarify what was agreed, how it was going to be achieved and by when.

- You will need to be able and willing to listen and show you are a people person when communicating with an I. They are happy to be sold to so long as you are fast paced and creative in your delivery, and don't over-do the detail.

S - Steadiness and communication

- When communicating with an S give lots of time to reflect so they can make any decisions required at a steady pace. Unlike an I, S's are more apt to listen than talk, but like an I they are people orientated. They don't like the direct and abrupt approach a high D can show which can come across to them as too combative.

- You will need to show your appreciation when communicating with an S. Even when they have high levels of competence and confidence S's will still be happier with a participative rather than telling or selling approach due to the importance they place on inclusive relationships.

C - Conscientious and communication

- When communicating with a C give lots of data and quality responses. Like a D they will want you to get straight to business, but unlike both the D and I they will want lots and lots of detail. Similar to an S they like lots of time, but for consideration and analysis, before making any decisions.

- You will need to show a precision of thought and approach when communicating with a C. They will want you to behave in a business-like and professional manner at all times. Communications should be written where possible. If there needs to be a one to one or team meetings have a pre-set agenda, followed up by clear action minutes. C's are happy with a telling approach, so long as this comes with precise instructions.

As we can see, communication does need to be reframed around individuals to best support organizational or business success in a much more sophisticated way than our previously and generally held assumptions has led us to believe.

It is important the communication strategy connects to staff and follower's intrinsic motivation for trust and respect, based on shared values and beliefs that allow individuals to get what they want – not what the leader thinks they want. There therefore needs to be scope for self-management connected to the organizations purpose, through a high competence base and a mechanism for recognizing and encouraging staff to be 'independent truth tellers.' Otherwise we are likely to set up the foundations for a culture where people focus on what can go wrong, not what they *can do*, which can easily spiral into the dreaded blame culture we discussed in section F.

We need to be careful here to distinguish between employee and follower as often change agents are employees rather than owners of businesses or bosses in organizations. At these points it is the owner or the boss who will become the follower.

It's long been accepted that asking open questions can facilitate deeper thinking and reflection required for raised self-awareness, a quality in high demand for any leader and more and more so we recognize its need for effective staff and followers. Many of us in the world of coaching and leadership will have incorporated open questions into our resource bank (such as 'what might...?', 'if you...?', 'in what way...?'). These are useful in expanding the Reality and Options stages in the GROW model. But people can often become 'stuck' when confronted by open questions, especially in situations where they have newly been incorporated into our way of working. This is especially true of people who have a number of limiting beliefs or assumptions that restrict the range of options, strategies, possibilities and creative solutions that sit outside their 'norm.'

It might be instructive to consider the notion of queer at this point. Historically queer was something strange and negative and latterly synonymous with a deviance model. Implicit in this approach was the 'assumption' that behavior belonged to the individual rather than a function of the social group. This shifted after the 1970s when the biological conception of sexuality was replaced with the notion of constructed sexuality that allowed for the appropriation of the term queer to donate one's strangeness (difference) positively.

The philosopher Judith Butler's notion of performativity came to be a key notion in queer theory (an iterative process of repetition). Gilles Deleuze and Felix Guattari extended this where, for them, you cannot *be* queer as queer is a becoming. This is a shift from being *in* the world to becoming *with* the world, which very much aligns to the developments in psychology John Whitmore discusses, and prefigures evolutionary organizational development from dependence, to independence, to interdependence (the old norming, storming, forming, performing organizational or team development we discussed in section H). This mirrors the coaching journey through the early stages of acceptance of our norms and assumptions (our limiting beliefs), to challenging those beliefs, forming new ways of seeing the world around us, and performing at new levels or excelling in new areas (reflecting our earlier discussion on repetitive practice for changing habits in section E - Gweck's Growth Model exemplifies this at the individual and at the team level, where change is inevitable, growth a choice).

Whitmore thinks the 'command and control' culture has 'systemized and dehumanized' us all. Queer theorists offer a theory of positive difference; a synthesis of difference and repetition to fight against this. Here the self who repeats is composed of a multiplicity of tiny egos, so is at each moment of repetition different from itself (absolute self-difference). The similarities here to the 'sub-personalities' Whitmore talks about is clear (we will expand on this in section T), as is the 'ceaseless creativity, learning and enjoyment' he advocates if we want coaching to support the development of 'a new social order.' A new social order driven by our new wise men and women in 'purposeful relationships' that will support us in letting go of old ways of thinking, feeling and doing, and practicing new ways through heightened self-reflection, self-awareness, self-knowledge and self-mastery by bringing together our left/right aspects (we will elaborate on this in section R and more fully expand in section X).

My key learning point:

It was about this time I came to realize I had fallen into an old pattern of repetition; of over 'intellectualizing', but not 'feeling' my learning. Thereby stopping myself from positively progressing.

We need to embrace the spirit of synthesis, where the whole is greater than the sum of the parts.

What is your key learning point?

Chapter Eighteen

R - Reframing Cultures

Most people will have heard the metaphor, "Is the glass half-full or half-empty?" Reframing, which facilitates positive change, does not actually change the situation. The glass will still have the same amount in it. Reframing changes our perception of the situation which in turn enables us to see alternative and more positive and productive ways of responding.

We mentioned in the last section the need for the development of deeper levels of thinking and reflection to help raise self-awareness. Reframing is a useful technique through which to do this, through challenging ourselves in our day to day situations as well as considering our generally unspoken and unconscious assumptions, beliefs and values. Framing, which we will expand on later in this section, is an effective shortcut for processing information. However, it is unfortunate that people in general, according to Susan T. Fiske and Shelley E. Taylor, are by nature "cognitive misers", meaning they prefer to do as little thinking as possible. So while framing is effective in one sense it also has the potential for hugely negative results when our perceptions are not fully thought through.

Remember those limiting beliefs we discussed in the Introduction? Reframing gives us a means to identify those perceptions, assumptions, beliefs and values that are no longer helpful in our lives, and allows us to replace them with more positive or adaptive ones, thereby turning problems into opportunities. This is a process that switches our too often 'negative feedback loop' into a 'positive feedback loop' that connect the left and right sides of the brain.

The notion of the left/right brain split is well known, with the left brain (sometimes known as the everyday self) being logical and linear. The so called 'objective' side that works from knowledge and that enables us to use language and speech. The right brain is the creative and abstract side. The right side works through stories, shape and pattern. This is the so called 'subjective' side that controls our emotions, feelings and energy. This understanding has major significance for focus and attention. As noted previously one of the key steps towards greater self-awareness is focused attention, and as previously mentioned our energy goes to where our focus is. With the huge demands on our attention from our daily lives is it any wonder we are such 'cognitive misers' with little left to cultivate a more positive and productive stance?

Getting our left and right brain to work to support one another is a powerful tool and we can see this through the reframing of emotional states, enabling more positivity and optimism. A well-known example of this is called 'bridging' where we use language (left brain) in this instance through the use of the word 'manageable/y' to help us control our emotional state (right brain);

- I feel depressed: The use of this statement locks us into that emotional state (that frame).
- I feel manageably depressed: This does not change the emotional state of being depressed, but it does give a sense of control over it.
- I feel manageable: This allows us to move from the feeling of depression and opens up the emotions to feeling something else (potential to shift the frame).
- I feel manageably happy: If you are open to feeling something else you are then able to accept being manageably happy.
- I feel happy: The use of this statement locks us into that emotional state (that frame). We have now reframed the original state of being 'depressed' to the state of being

'happy.'

You are now in a position where you can change the word used from 'manageable/y' to 'increasingly' to extend the emotional state you now feel.

- I feel increasingly happy: Now you open yourself up to the possibilities of feeling even more than happy.

This has real significance for the development of emotional intelligence, i.e. knowing one's emotions, which as we know is the foundations of self-awareness, because once we accept and understand this process (from a left brain position) we are then able to work more creatively and cooperatively with the right brain - creating synergy.

Let's look at the what we mean by 'framing.' Framing theory is about how individuals, groups, and societies, organize, perceive, and communicate about 'their' reality, placing their reality within a field of meaning. So framing is about giving meaning to something that would otherwise be meaningless. This inevitably leads to framing bias where we present our reality as fact, but which is in fact skewed towards a certain viewpoint. This has huge significance as it undermines our previously held belief in 'rational choice theory', where we believed that people were rational beings who would make consistent choices based on consistent data. We now know this not to be the case. Indeed, work in the neurosciences shows us that framing takes place in the amygdala and the orbital and medial prefrontal cortex (OMPFC) which moderates the role of the emotions. When greater activity is taking place in the OMPFC (so related to the emotions rather than rationality) we are less susceptible to framing effects. Or put differently we are more susceptible to framing effects when emotions are less engaged, i.e. when we are so called more rational. Our choices therefore have been shown to be dependent on our current frame.

Framing theory was originally put forward by Erving Goffman who showed that people interpret what is going on for them through a primary framework that is 'taken for granted.' George Lakoff then carried out work showing the difficulties of counteracting an established frame with his now famous directive 'Don't think of an elephant!' However, once you have been given a directive not to think about an elephant it is almost impossible not to think about an elephant. This is due, Lakoff says, to four morals:

- Moral 1. Every word evokes a frame (so the word elephant evokes the image of an elephant).
- Moral 2: Words defined within a frame evoke the frame (e.g. trunk in this context evokes an elephant).
- Moral 3: Negating a frame evokes the frame (don't think about an elephant evokes the image of an elephant).
- Moral 4: Evoking a frame reinforces that frame.

The important point is that every time a frame is evoked in the brain by neural circuitry it strengthens that neural circuit (i.e. that frame), so think back to our reframing example of 'manageable/y' to counter our old frame of depression and strengthen a new one of being happy. When we understand that emotions develop in the front part of the brain and move backward in the brain as they are processed, while on the other hand, the emotional reappraisal process begins in the back of the brain and moves forward, we can see connections to our earlier discussion on synergy with reframing our emotions, thinking and behavior. And further this connects 'imagery techniques' in psychosynthesis and other therapeutic work that can strengthen a more positive and productive view of our world.

My key learning point:

Having come to understand the resurfacing of my old pattern of intellectualizing over feeling I began to see my own nature as an 'emotional miser' and the need to reframe my need for safety through distance to a life of engagement.

We need to reframe our emotional and thinking and behavioral responses before we can feel, think or act differently.

What is your key learning point?

_____

_____

_____

_____

_____

_____

Chapter Nineteen

S - Safer Culture

In this age of new technology, the internet has become an invaluable tool for businesses across the globe. Sitting alongside this however cybercrime and e-safety have become major concerns for many organizations. Cyber expert Gary Hibberd, while recognizing that cybercrime is a threat to businesses, thinks we need to take a pragmatic risk-based approach; use different passwords, ensure your anti-virus and firewall software is up to date and working, stop sharing so much information with others and become more online savvy. For many, cybercrime should be the least of our worries as leaders and business owners.

We hear much about the changing nature of work, where everyone is shifting from being a customer to becoming a supplier of something or other. In the future, we are told, few of the current roles and industries we take for granted will exist. As technology develops and employee expectations around flexible working arrangements continue an increase in businesses virtual infrastructures can be expected to continue to expand. Some key questions therefore might be; what impact will this changing approach to how we service our business, customer and staffing needs have on the culture of our organizations and businesses? How do we safeguard a culture of collaboration and success? Indeed, how do we safeguard the very existence of our businesses?

If Charles Handy is correct we might need to consider that we are at (or have we already passed?) the point of 'the second curve.' For some this will seem like a great opportunity. But for many, if not most, this will send them directly into the area of ambiguity and uncertainty we discussed in Section B and followed up in Section E. Change as we have already noted is not easy, and indeed that is really an understatement. There are many books and articles which offer change management strategies, rarely however do they admit to being partially successful at best. Yet we know that businesses are continually failing to recognize the need for change or change quickly enough when the need is recognized.

So let's relook at change. We know historically change took place over large spans of time, while today change and especially change driven by new technologies is occurring at an accelerated pace. This has taken us from a world view of a stable order to one of shifting relationships and ambiguity as noted above. Indeed, this shift fits well with our understanding of DISC which sees our personality traits in relation to our environment, so aligning individual change to social and cultural change.

We can now see from the new developments in neuroscience and especially in relation to neuroculture that everything we believe is created in the brain. Therefore, how we map our thoughts, which are a biological function, to our behavior when responding to our environment is now more easily understood. This was foreseen in Dr. William Marston's DISC Model through the *Emotions of Normal People*. We now know that brain characteristics are common across all societies. What is different is the cultural interpretations we put on the 'facts' which throw into relief our values and beliefs.

Cultural theories abound, as do theories around cultural change. Whichever theory you ascribe to, the important thing is the clear connection that exists between culture and values, and so our beliefs, which explains the enduring nature of culture and the difficulty we find in sustaining many change initiatives

Key fact – 75% of change initiatives fail.

The lack of sustainability in many change initiatives is due to too great a focus on the change management process itself rather than the underlying cultural values and beliefs that will support or undermine the need for and sustainability of change. This aligns well to the Gestalt approach, as advocated by Fredrick Perls through his Paradoxical Theory of Change. For Perls "change occurs when one becomes what he is, not when he tries to become what he is not." This is equivalent to the focused attention we have spoken of before. Not a focus on the change or the 'trying' to change, rather a focus on who we fully are in order to gain a 'firm footing' from which to move. There are lots of ways to drive cultural change, but as we can see without addressing our underlying values and beliefs thereby gaining our 'firm footing' changes are unlikely to be effective or sustainable over the long term.

Thomas R. Rochon in *Culture Moves: Ideas, Activism and Changing Values* articulated the flow of cultural and social movements, where new ideas and values take hold in the public's mind through the media. In light of this we might want to question what impact the internet is having on culture. The sociologist Frank Furedi says, "There is little doubt that digital technology and social media has already had a significant impact on culture" citing the examples of social protest and mobilization of resistance. Here we can see the practical bringing together of the virtual and the real, which has now become part and parcel of the 'reality' of contemporary everyday cultures.

On a more significant scale we can see the impact new technology can have on culture when we consider this in relation to genetics. If we reflect back, we will remember that change can happen overnight if we can get people to believe in new ideas/ myths (this stands at odds with the rest of the animal kingdom who require change at the genetic level for social change to occur). However, with the developments in bioengineering, cybernetics and inorganic life there is the potential to separate culture from our biological developments completely. Raising the questions; just how safe are our cultures? And how proactive are we being in cultivating the positive and productive cultures we really desire and deserve?

My key learning point:

Having accepted my own culpability in my own mindless dash for change I am now better placed to support positive purposeful change in myself and others.

We need to embrace the paradox of change.

What is your key learning point?

Chapter Twenty

T - Transpersonal Cultures

Roberto Assagioli, founder of psychosynthesis, says,

"Everything is spiritual that relates to the unfoldment or true progression of humanity."

Will Parfitt, psychotherapist and author of *'Psychosynthesis'* says there is no point getting in touch with the spiritual unless there is going to be some practical application related to our intentions (i.e. getting our deeper needs fulfilled). But what are those deeper needs? Do we mean the needs of each of our personality styles; for the D's to be in charge, for the I's to have recognition, for the S's to have appreciation, and for the C's to have excellence? Or are we talking about something else – if so, what?

Let's take a step back first and ask the questions; What is psychosynthesis? And what does this mean in a business context?

Psychosynthesis is often described as a route to self-realization. One that is highly practical. Assagioli says, "Psychosynthesis is a method of psychological development and self-realization for those who refuse to remain the slaves of their own inner phantasms or of external influences, who refuse to submit passively to the play of psychological forces which is going on within them, and who are determined to become the master of their lives." Psychosynthesis then is concerned with exploring our psychology and our spirituality in a practical sense that brings value to our daily life. It is a form of transpersonal psychology (dealing with the material and the immaterial; the mind and the spirit).

From a practical perspective psychosynthesis focuses on the

individual to 'know yourself' and how the individual interacts within the group and their environment. This correlates well with DISC which remember is about raising awareness of our 'default' personality traits and so behaviors in interactions and environments, and whether we perceive those environments to be favorable or unfavorable, and have power to change or control the environment.

So, to answer the question what does this mean in a business context, we only need consider how this fits with improved communications, motivation, responsibility and ownership. And at a deeper level what this would mean for setting core values, beliefs and goals. These are all key to business success and will be even more so as we progress into our networked age with heightened expectations around 'why' we do business, and 'who' we do business with, where pure profit is not enough and the quadruple bottom-line (people, profit, planet and sustainable progress) takes precedence.

One of the issues often perceived to exist in the business world is the drive for the rational. An unemotional stance to practical business decisions (left brain thinking). This outdated mode of thinking still prevails, yet we know that it is emotions, not the intellect or rational thinking, that drives most of our actions. Think back to our discussion around cortisol, oxytocin and dopamine which act as biological triggers that drive our emotions. Indeed, if we expand on the connection between biology and the brain we now know that first and foremost we are driven by our instincts through the reptilian part of the brain (brain stems and cerebellum). This is the drive for survival and reproduction. We then have the limbic system which drives our emotions, and this system is full of contradictions (we will return to this when we discuss the notion of sub-personalities). And finally we have the cortex which is the area that handles learning and the development of logic. However, this part of the brain is not put to any practical use until after the age of seven by which time most of our beliefs and values have been set. So biology sets out our basic parameters (your 'default' personality). It is this more than anything that illustrates the need for high levels of self-awareness, to support self-mastery for the cultivation of positive and productive cultures.

However, we need to be careful not to work under the mistaken assumption that when we talk about culture we are always talking about something big and external to ourselves, i.e. thinking that culture is out there. Culture is in fact every bit internal as it is external.

A client had come to me for coaching, ostensibly to support her with issues around time management. When she said she was 'stuck' I asked her, "What would your mother say?"

"Too much. I'm sick of her niggly voice in my head."

"Under what circumstances does her voice show up?" I asked.

"When I'm dithering or stuck," the client said "she's there nagging. It's like she just can't abide me not knowing what to do."

"What does she want right now?" I asked.

"She wants me to stop procrastinating. She always wants that. She always did and I'm sick of it. Well I'm stuck and I'm staying stuck."

I have mentioned on a number of occasions now that strange notion of sub-personalities. What are these? The easiest way to think about this might be to envisage a team. Some of who communicate better than others. Some are more dominant, some more friendly, some more supportive, some more critical. Some try to please while some don't care, some are somber and reflective, some are carefree and erratic. The job of a leader and manager is to motivate teams of disparate people to work well together to achieve a common goal (remember we talked about positive energy flow). When this works well there are high levels of congruence and success. When it doesn't there can be dissonance, conflict and underachievement.

If you now transplant this notion into your own mind your sub-personalities are your own internal team which work well together or are in conflict. Your job is to bring these sub-personalities together to work in alignment to achieve your goal. This is where it is of absolute priority that you know your own values, beliefs and purpose, for if you don't know your core 'why' you will not be in a position to bring understanding and direction to your competing sub-personalities.

The notion of sub-personalities has come out of a range of humanistic psychologies, such as, Roberto Assagioli's Psychosynthesis, where we are engaged in "a continual effort, conscious or not, to establish equilibrium" between the different part of us that want different things (i.e. our sub-personalities). Or Carl Jung's notion of Archetypes (although references to archetypes can be traced back as far as Plato who talked about the fundamental characteristics of things imprinted on the soul). For Jung there are a number of key archetypes, such as "the shadow, the wise old man, the child, the mother ... and her counterpart, the maiden, and lastly the anima in man and the animus in woman." Archetypes are the mediators between the psychic realm and reality, meaning they govern our behavior through pre-set psycho-physical patterns. These patterns drive the individual and so drive culture.

Sub-personalities should not be confused with multiple personality disorder which is a medical condition. Our sub-personalities are a natural state of affairs (albeit one that most of us have spent very little time paying attention to). A point to bear in mind is that while these sub-personalities (inner voices) appear to be negative they are actually doing so with positive intentions. They were initially created to help you in some way when they were needed. They are not your enemy, but a part of you that needs to be understood, accepted and integrated (remember we discussed motivation and whether your motivational drives were supporting or hindering you? You will be unable to answer this question until you understand your sub-personalities).

Whether we think about archetypes and shadow selves, or sub-personalities there will be a number of core patterns of behavior which revolve around the hero/warrior, sage/teacher, jester, lover, victim, rebel, caregiver, creator to name but a few. The key point is not to rid ourselves of our sub-personalities but to better connect to them and bring them into the light of day. We do this through identifying and 'naming' them (for the purpose of then being better able to dis-identify with them). This is an important and difficult point to grasp, but without dis-identification we are not able to choose which aspect of our personality is the most appropriate for a given situation. So if we refer back to DISC and whether we see our environment as friendly or hostile and whether we can control the environment or not, we can see that this state of dis-identification is required to shift our 'default' position.

If we expand this out to the cultural level of an organization, and refer back to Jung's collective unconscious, which has been called the 'organizational unconscious', the practices that convey the true (i.e. operational) values of the organization rather than the aspirational values we like to write up on our plaques and in our strategy documents we can really see the complexities and similarities between organizational and individual culture. So to go right back to our question at the start of this book, which comes first the chicken or the egg? We can now see that the inter-relationship between the macro and the micro, and the intrarela-tionships within the micro itself, necessitates an intervention of great significance if we wish to derail and redirect either.

Further, this then answers the perennial question; is culture something an organization has (something you can change) or something it is (something you can only understand but not change)? Peters and Waterman wrote *In Search of Excellence*

"Without exception the dominance and coherence of culture proved to be an essential quality of the excellent companies." So cultures may change slowly in the normal course of events, but with an intervention of some significance the pace can be stepped up and new values, beliefs and so new habits (new cultures) formed.

Self-reflection

You might want to reflect on the following questions;

- Can you identify any patterns of behavior you have in different or specific situations?
- Can you 'name' any of these as types or sub-personalities?
- Which one/s do you find most helpful?
- Which one/s do you find most disruptive?

My key learning point:

It was while in counselling for the first time that I came across the strange notion of archetypes and shadow selves, out of which came my understanding of my 'two families' that shaped my erratic drive for continual change.

We need to identify and 'name' our sub-personalities so we can then dis-identify with them.

What is your key learning point?

_____

_____

_____

_____

_____

_____

Chapter Twenty-one

U - Understanding Cultures

The answer that I cannot find
Is known to my unconscious mind.
I have no reason to despair
Because I am already there.
The Maze - Auden

Coaching is a means to unlock those secret vaults through asking powerful and incisive questions, which Colin Wilson said "jolt us out of our collective trance", for the purpose of challenging the 'crazy' notion that we can continue to do what we always have and yet get different results (whether that be continually strive to be the same or continually strive to be different). We first need to understand this, in line with the paradox of change, if we wish to cultivate a more positive and productive culture.

So what is our understanding now of culture?

We know culture is an imagined reality. We know that imagined realities give us meaning that stop us falling into the void – what has been called the 'existential emptiness.' This is a really important point as it counters the otherwise meaningless of life; the eternal 'No.' We now know that a lack of meaning and purpose are among the most destructive states we can experience. Yet much of our modern cultural norms have descended into a negativity that makes it all but impossible to channel our positive life energy, where daily life exhausts our attention, and to quote Colin Wilson again "drains our vital batteries."

We know that the dominant culture in too many organizations is still command and control, which in turn sits within a larger cultural setting that has been constructed through ideology of those in positions of power. And we know that this ideology has shifted from predominantly class based to a shared mentality between a disparate elite that have managed (albeit unconsciously) to convince the vast majority of people of the lack of alternatives.

This tells us then that culture is not static and that there are alternatives. However, it also shows us that for any significant shift to take place there is a need for a concerted, prolonged and collective drive in order to counter current cultural norms that "has left many people resigned, devoid of hope, without a feeling that it is possible to resist" to quote Owen Jones. And this is where the great difficulties arise.

- We live in a world too full of distractions, deflection and misdirection where it is only too easy not to see what is right in front of our eyes.
- We are by nature 'cognitive misers' and are only too happy not to think through things that do not already conform to what we believe.
- We lack an understanding of our energy flow and so are unable to sustain focused attention.
- Through extensive use our left brains have become stronger, while our right brains have grown weaker. This has made it difficult for us to even consider alternatives.
- Psychologically we cling to our 'passionate attachment' to those in power and fear the responsibility that would come with letting this go.
- We are prone to denial and self-deception which enables us to justify our false consciousness.

**Nietzsche said "If you have a 'why' to live,
you can bear almost any 'how'."**

But is this really how we want to live? If we want to do anything about our current situation and impact on the culture we find ourselves in, we might start by asking:

- What is my purpose?
- What is the hunger I am here to feed?
- What is important to me as opposed to what is urgent?
- What is it that makes *this* important to me?
- How will my current course of actions contribute to the achievement of my goals?
- Or, what do I want from work other than the pay?

These are great questions to enable you to move from a place of being 'stuck' to a place of understanding and so becoming unstuck. What might this mean for our four main DISC personality types?

Dominant

Some key issues a D might present are fear of failure or losing control especially on 'big' projects and projects in new areas not experienced before, difficulties in building effective relationships and getting the team on board in a new role or organization, or struggling to create a cohesive culture across different aspects of the team (especially after a merger). You can take a very pragmatic approach to this, which many D's would, and address each of these issues one by one and head-on. In all likelihood the issues will, to all intents and purposes, be solved. However, the larger 'why' will not have been addressed and so the issues will be perennial. And so while the organization or business may well be successful it will still never reach its full potential and will continue to address emerging issues that could well have been addressed once and for all at the root.

Influencer

Some key issues an I might present are fear of conflict or

being disliked. As a people person this can be very difficult to handle. Losing control of the detail is a worry for high I's with a good level of self-awareness as they realize this is not their natural strong point. I's should have no difficulties in building effective relationships and getting the team on board but may have issues around sustaining this as others may expect more and more of their time and positivity. If this is not forth-coming, they could be perceived as 'inauthentic.' For an I there should be an easiness in the relationship with others to be able to explain this perceptual difference. And if they are smart they will get a high C on board to cover the detail. These will go some way to address the personal 'why' but will not address the core 'why' in the organization. This is why it is important to understand organizational as well as individual personality.

Steadiness

Some key issues an S might present are fear of change and high risk situations, again this could be on 'big' projects and projects in new areas not experienced before. Equally, after a merger there could be real worries of competitiveness, aggression and confrontation. An overly supportive approach at these times could be perceived by others as weak and lacking authority that could develop into that 'toxic' cocktail' we mentioned earlier. Nevertheless, as S's are natural people people who love order and certainty they can often bring a friendly and harmonious order to what at first appears disordered. The trick though is to enable this feeling of order to persist in what is nowadays a fast paced, change orientated world. This is why it is highly important for high S's to have a clarity around their own and the organizations 'why' or they will be continually having to readdress the issues of uncertainty and ambiguity.

Conscientious

Some key issues a C might present are the fear of being seen as not knowing what to do, not doing things correctly or allowing standards to drop, and so an overriding fear of criticism. This is particularly pertinent when on tight deadlines, on high stake projects, projects in new areas and in other pressurized environments. A C's approach to this could be to tighten the reins further, slip into micromanagement, and create a culture of intimidation and judging where others can never measure up to expected standards. This can inadvertently lead to the blame game. C's with a good level of self-awareness will balance this with lots of praise, a conscious effort to lighten up and a recognition that perfection does not exist. Nevertheless, without a good understanding of the organizations core 'why' you can find slippage back to doing things right rather than a clear focus on doing the right thing.

We will continue then to replay our issues if we do not tap into our internal vault, our knowledge that we keep locked away through being such 'cognitive and emotional misers.' The question though is how do we do this in a deep and sustained way that not only transforms ourselves but the cultures we find ourselves in.

I have already mentioned the need to develop our left brain right brain dialogue to create synergy between our logical and linear and creative and abstract selves. There is much debate as to whether there is a left/right brain split, or whether this is a myth and there is a natural interplay between the two sides. This argument misses the point, which is that through repetitive use or lack of use different aspects become stronger or weaker respectively. What is required is a bringing of the interplay between the left and right parts of the brain into conscious awareness to strengthen our ability to engage in the interplay.

It is interesting if we consider this from an evolutionary perspective we know that Cro-Magnon man of 200,000 years ago worshiped a 'oneness with the universe' – a very right brain perspective. It wasn't until a mere 1,200 years BC that things changed. It is unclear why this might be. It has been suggested this was due to the great volcanic eruptions of Santorini, or to radiation from a comet 12P/Pons-Brooks. Either way the evidence is clear that by 1,200 BC our ancestors had become more left brain orientated resulting in violence, invasion and a growing impatience that has driven what we now call 'scientific thought' where we doubt everything.

This drive towards scientific thought inevitable led to Kant's philosophical two worlds 'phenomenon' and 'neumenon'; directly accessible to observation and not directly accessible to observation. Descartes and the Existentialists continued down this mistaken road. It was Johann Gottlieb Fichte who questioned this, saying that if something is not directly accessible to observation we should ignore it, and so all there is is phenomenon, in which case "man is left in a world created by his senses...But if 'I' really created the universe, why do I not know that I did? There must be two 'me's', this everyday self who has no idea of what is going on, and another 'me' who is actually a kind of god who has created this world", as Colin Wilson notes in *Super Consciousness*. This gives us a much more positive and active existentialism where "human beings do possess freedom, but most of the time they waste it by living robotically", but nevertheless gives us a route map to become more free (self-actualization) through tapping into positive energy flow coming out of the interplay between our left/right brain, or a will to consciousness. Indeed, this connects to Jung's 'collective unconscious', Maslow's 'peak experience' and Roberto Assagioli's psychosynthesis that seeks to bring together the 'self' and the 'Self' where we work "with the personality to the expansion of consciousness into the greater Self" as Stephanie Sowell put it in *Psychosynthesis*, thereby gaining a sense of being part of something greater than oneself.

Throughout this book I have steered clear of the overtly political, but when discussing leadership, organizational development and the quadruple bottom-line it is not possible, or indeed advisable, to dodge the truly political aspect of our endeavor. I believe it is reprehensible that 'we' have allowed our culture to become as negative as it currently is, our politics to be dominated by such a small coterie of mega-elite, and to support an economic set-up that advocated 'no alternative' to, as Owen Jones notes in *The Establishment*, "1,000 individuals worth £520 billion, while hundreds of thousands of people have to queue to eat in food banks."

Leadership in our command and control dominated society is epitomized by strong characters such as Margaret Thatcher, Sir Alan Sugar and more latterly Donald Trump; straight talking, hard-headed and at times bullying and fairly obnoxious characters. What we might call high intensity D's with little to no self-awareness. This is by no means to diminish the achievements of any one of these as individuals, but if we do want to change society and our culture for the better these leadership traits can no longer be seen as appropriate for a networked and distributed future in which we can all participate on a more egalitarian basis.

You might question what this has to do with left/right brain thinking, our psychological make-up, evolutionary development and philosophical speculation. But the connection couldn't be clearer. Earlier I had mentioned the need to shift from an ego centered mentality. This is a shift from an 'I – It' where we see others as objects, to an 'I – Thou' dynamic where we see both ourselves and others as subjects. The great educationalist Paulo Freire talks about our binary approach to people; as objects, so moldable and malleable; and as subjects, so independent and able to transcend and recreate the world. For the shift from object to subject thinking to have any impact though it needs to be married to a technology of practice (remember we talked earlier about repetition and practice makes permanent). So we need to find new rituals and routines that connect reframing, through 'bridging', to a better working and synergy of the left/right brain interplay.

Self-reflection

You might want to reflect on these questions;

- When was the last time you purposefully thought new thoughts?
- What might be the consequences of thinking new thoughts on a regular basis?
- When was the last time you questioned your own thinking pattern?
- Have you ever noticed falling into self-deception? Or are you too far in denial for that?
- What might be the outcome of recognising, accepting and questioning self-deception in yourself?

My key learning point:

My own passionate attachments, denial and periods of self-deception have been too many and manifest to list. Coaching has been invaluable for challenging these, but this has by no means been an easy or comfortable journey. But it has been a necessary one.

We need to challenge our own thinking and justification processes.

What is your key learning point?

_____

_____

_____

_____

_____

Chapter Twenty-two

V - Visionary Cultures

Visionaries have variously been described as those who envision a better future, those who are imaginative, creative and inspired. Or characterized as those who take flights of fancy, lack practical insight and are 'pejoratively' seen as eccentric or downright mad. Much has been written about our mad geniuses, our eccentric revolutionaries and our spiritual romantics, invariably contrasting the two poles noted above. The conclusion being that visionaries tend to be unable to bring a balance to their high ideals and aspirations with the realities of day to day life. This is highly convenient for all those practical left brainers and a true warning to all those flighty right brainers, but does little to bring understanding to the great untapped potential of a left/right brain synergy. When we consider back to our zoning discussion (comfort, stretch and panic) and align this to our tendency to be 'cognitive misers' this is not really surprising. Nevertheless, this is exactly what needs to be challenged.

We are learning so much more about who we are, why we do things, leadership styles and organizational development through the advances in neuroscience, psychology and other research and development work. You only have to consider Daniel Goleman and his colleagues work on their six leadership styles; with visionary, coaching, affiliative and democratic being the four styles seen as leading to harmony, positivity and longevity of success. While commanding and pacesetting (our old command and control favorites) are seen as only really useful in crisis management situations. Visionary leaders are seen to epitomize Mahatma Gandhi's "You must be the change you wish to see in the world" through being truly people orientated and concerned first and foremost with making the world a better place for others. This is an important point. Visionaries focus on people, not projects, tasks or profits. This leaves us in a real quandary when we try and equalize the leadership potential of all our DISC types. Or at least it does until we refer back to our discussions around self-awareness, adaptability and blends.

"Some men see things as they are and ask, why; I dream things that never were and ask, why not." This is a quote that I believe comes from George Bernard Shaw, but which I first came across on a card my Step-Gran sent to me many many years ago. My Step-Gran had been a fiery and scary, woman. She was the first woman on the Scottish National Party's National Executive. Remember this was the 1960s when feminism may have helped secure the 'pill' but equality of the sexes was light-years away; a time when the SNP was only really beginning to have any recognizable impact; and a time when Scotland itself was only beginning to reawaken, as emphasized by the now famous Winnie Ewing quote on the night of her by-election victory, "stop the world, Scotland wants to get on."

Looking back my Step-Gran had epitomized for me everything a great visionary should be; she had a purpose, energy and determination to make the world a better place. She introduced me to art, politics and the love of learning. But unfortunately she also had something else, a building commitment to the 'demon drink' that turned her idealism into cynicism, her empathy into contempt and her persuasiveness into preaching. She had been unable to reconcile her visionary ideals with the let downs of daily life. And I saw in her, reflections of who I would become.

We have discussed at length our four key DISC personality traits and types and covered some of the blends, especially our D/I I/D, I/S S/I, S/C C/S, and C/D D/C, but let's take some time to consider some less typical blends and what this might mean for those who wish to develop their visionary potential (what I am suggesting is the ability to bring together your left/right brain).

D/I/C (Dominant/Influencer/ Conscientious) Blend

- We already know that a D/I person tends to be direct, take control and be inspired to have fun. I's in particular are happy to connect to the imaginative and creative right side of the brain. If we add to this a high level of C a person with this blend is likely to want to do this while paying close attention to detail and quality. This is a heady combination that would require a good level of self-awareness and openness to enable them to pay attention to other people's feelings, engage in empathy, and focus on a bigger purpose than profit if they want to benefit from the potential for left/right brain balance.

C/D/S (Conscientious/ Dominant/ Steadiness) Blend

- We already know that a C/D person tends to be highly task focused, detailed orientated and expects high standards. If we add to this a high level of S there tends to be a sensitivity to other people's needs. However, at times this can be sidelined with the two task focused aspects. These types then can become analytical with their relationships rather than close. They tend to work from a logical left brained approach where 'the facts' are all that matter. It can be difficult for people with this blend to see the need for right brain integration and so a high level of self-challenge would be necessary.

C/S/D (Conscientious/ Steadiness/ Dominant) Blend

- We know that C/S people tend to be reliable and methodical in their approach and like predictability. However, due to their compliant nature they can lack flexibility and are unlikely to go against the norm. The addition of D can give these people a boost to their self-esteem, but can lead to a distance from people issues to the exclusion of the task. These blends are not great at embracing new ideas and would need to challenge their openness, confidence and imagination if they desired to better connect their left/right brains.

S/D or D/S (Steadiness/ Dominant) Blend

* People with this blend tend to be intense and hard working. They are strong completers, but can be impatient with others who cannot meet their demanding expectations. They will tend to be highly focused, but can be linear and lacking in imagination. Indeed, they can become frustrated with others who veer of the set path. It would be a real challenge for this type to take on a right brain approach without lots of support and practice.

I/C or C/I (Influencer/ Conscientious) Blend

* This is an unusual blend that can result in outgoing people who can still be analytical and cautious. These types tend to be friendly, caring and quite adaptable. If the I is intense enough these people can be comfortable expressing their thoughts and emotions, being creative and logical. The trick for these blends is to enable their naturally left/right brain dialogue to coexist and not fall into 'should' thinking. If they can carry this off they have the ability to be highly influential. At the same time, they need to curb their potential for hypersensitivity. However, combined this has the potential for these blends to be powerful leaders.

D/I/S/C (Dominant/ Influencer/ Steadiness/ Conscientious)

* But what about a healthy interplay of all four personality

traits? Robert A. Rohm in his book *Positive Personality Profiles* suggests that Jesus Christ "displayed the truly integrated and complete personality which God purposed for mankind." Jesus could be a demanding D (consider his dramatic actions in the Temple), an inspirational I (think about his act of let's talk, let's eat when he turned seven loaves and fishes into enough for a whole crowd), a supportive S servant of the people (did he not clean the feet of his Disciples and welcome the small children), and a critical questioning C (remember how he turned the tables on the Scribes and Pharisees?) We could just as easily learn from Buddha, with his determined doer approach of a D, the good humor that abounds in Buddhism of a clear I, the tolerance and kindness of a high S, and the contemplative C. Or Muhammad who was driven and determined as any D to spread God's revelations, being an inducing cause agent in true I style, with the diplomacy of an S (such as laying of the Black Stone), and the compliance of a C such as the drafted of the Constitution of Medina.

Clearly we can't all be a Christ, a Buddha or a Muhammad but visionaries come in all shapes and sizes and in all walks of life. You only have to think of the great scientist Albert Einstein, the civil rights activists Martin Luther King and the Pankhursts. Or contemporaries such as, the Dalai Lama, with a righteous ambition of a high D, the optimism of an I, the immeasurable humility of an S and the conscientiousness of a C. Or Richard Branson with his high D business acumen, inspirational and fun loving I, philanthropic ventures typical of an S, and in true C style it is said he diarizes by the minute. Or what of Malala Yousafzai, the Pakistani schoolgirl who has been speaking out for women's right to education. She has shown the determination of a D, the positivity of an I, the patience of an S and the discipline of a C. Indeed, anyone who dares to be different in this left brain dominated world can practice left/right brain dialogues to support strengthening, adapting and adjusting our personality traits to please our "neighbour for his good, to build him up." An act Robert A. Rohm calls "his 'win-win' situation."

The confidence to be able to strengthen, adapt or adjust our traits to be that powerful and visionary person, to a great extent, comes with the control you feel you have over the environment and future outcomes. This relates quite specifically to Dr. Marston's questions as to how favorable you perceive your environment to be and how much control you feel you have over it. If we connect this to how adaptive you are able to be based on your openness to a growth mentality; how much effort you are willing to put in to raising or bringing forth your self-awareness (i.e. countering our natural state as a 'cognitive and emotional miser'); and how willing you are to shift from a 'skeptical materialism' – the scientific approach we have all been schooled and socialized into accepting, i.e. our left brain dominance to the detriment of our right brain aspects through what has been termed the 'disenchantment of modernity.' If we are open, willing and able to embrace these aspects we have the potential for a 'practical visionary' mechanism that can move us towards cultivating a more positive and productive culture that can transform us all.

My key learning point:

Fighting my own demons and reliving many of them while working through this book has turned my cynicism into compassion, my impractical romanticism into creative conviction, and my surrendered difference to a 'me' I no longer knew into an enthusiastic, confident and more controlled 'I'.

We already have our own answers embedded in our own stories.

What is your key learning point?

_____

_____

_____

_____

_____

_____

Chapter Twenty-three

W - Win-Win Cultures

Do you work from abundance or scarcity? Do you nurture others strengths or fear them? Do you work the parts or have an inclusive approach that emphasizes the whole being greater than the sum of the parts? Does 1+1= ½, 1½, 2, or 3 and above? (as Stephen Covey asks in his book *7 Habits of Highly Effective People*) This is similar to asking, do you have an aggressive, compromising, transactional or a creative co-operational stance? These are all key questions in our pursuit for win-win, where we strengthen, adapt and adjust our personality traits to please our "neighbour for his good, to build him up" through transforming ourselves first to transform the world we live in.

I mentioned during the Introduction the quadruple bottom-line, a phrase that initially came from John Elkington's triple bottom-line, elaborated on in his 1997 book *Cannibals With Forks: The Triple Bottom Line Of 21st Century Business* to describe the separate social and environmental as well as financial 'bottom-lines' companies should be working to. We are now in the era of the quadruple bottom-line, what is often called the 4P's; people, planet, profit and sustainability for future generations (i.e. progress). Although many an astute reader will probably be able to add some more.

So what do we mean by this?

People refer to the well-being of employees and stakeholders as well as business practices towards labour and the communities we work within. Planet refers to environmental practices and the need to minimize any harmful impact, often referred to as reducing our ecological footprint, taking responsibility and bearing the brunt/cost for associated problems. Neither of the two aspects above undermine the need for businesses, or indeed individuals, to make a profit. However, profit needs to be seen as both internal and external - so benefiting the communities or societies we do business in. Sustainability for future generations (progress) has been defined by The Worldwatch Institute in their book *State of the world 2012: Creating sustainable prosperity* as "a result of sustainable development that enables all human beings to live with their basic needs met, with their dignity acknowledged, and with abundant opportunity to pursue lives of satisfaction and happiness, all without risk of denying others in the present and the future the ability to do the same." This definition puts human beings at the center of sustainability and indeed runs counter to much of what is currently taken as accepted practice. The core of this aspect is the need for 'adaptive innovation' in each of the three previous aspects of people, planet and profit, as well as the need for innovation in being innovative for sustainable future progress.

However, the gist of this book is individual personal development, leadership development and organizational development rather than business development. Win-win therefore in this context is about the transformation of the self to drive the transformation of our businesses to support the transformation of the world around us.

But why would we wish to transform ourselves? For me that goes back to our discussion in section H on compassion and relates to that old fashioned notion of neighbourliness. "Say not to your neighbor, Go, and come again, and tomorrow I will give; when you have it by you" *(Proverbs 3:28-35, The Bible)*. The Bible has neighbourliness as the second most important of the two great commandments, which connected neighbourliness to compassion and humility, coming from a place of sincerity, that leads to direct and positive action; 'actions speak louder than words.' In the Bible anyone and everyone is our neighbour; friends, strangers and enemies alike. It is not good enough to be selective in who we act neighbourly towards. Indeed, the general principle of good neighbourliness has been incorporated into international law which, to quote the *Yale Law Journal*, "obligates states to try to reconcile their interests with the interests of neighboring states."

So a true win-win for us all is when we can connect our personal to the global; connecting the trust and relationship building we discussed in section H at the individual and interpersonal level, with the purposeful energy flow we discussed in section T at the intrapersonal level, to secure transformation at the international (global) level for a purpose bigger than the self. This aligns to concepts in psychosynthesis where we connect the self (our personality, our 'I' through raised self-awareness) to the Self (our intrapsychic, spiritual aspect). When we can connect the 'I' and the Self we gain a sense of being part of something greater than oneself. This is equivalent to the AA's belief, which many might have heard of, 'a power greater than ourselves.'

This takes us far from the traditional self-absorption too many of us live our lives through, driven by an individualism that has shaped our cultures for the worse and that had led inevitably to the negative and meaninglessness of much of modern life and culture. What I referred to earlier as 'existential emptiness' rather than to a positive existentialism, the roots of which connect back all the way to the great Hermetic Alchemist Hermes Trismegistus. It is interesting that it was the Hermetic that repudiated the authority of the priest (for the early Christian tradition in the West there are only two sources of Power, the divine or the demonic, where the exercise of power that was not officially sanctioned 'could only, by definition, be demonic'). The Hermetic offered the basis from which to shift man's orientation from that of a passive to an active role, introducing the beginnings of man as an active agent. They would be aghast to find their efforts had led to man as 'individual' rather than as an 'interconnected oneness' (as above, so below).

My key learning point:

Researching and writing this book has enabled me to reconnect with my earlier artwork. Much of which had been themed around alcohol misuse, interconnectedness and moral action. The purpose of which was to critique a cultural shift from 'how we ought to live', to regulated behavior that suited territorial ends that has made slaves and captives of us all.

Knowing our purpose is insufficient, we must live our purpose. That is the true win-win.

What is your key learning point?

_____

_____

_____

_____

_____

_____

Chapter Twenty-four

X - Xenagogue Cultures

The great guides throughout the history of the human race have been the greatest of story-tellers.

Jesus Christ, Buddha, Muhammad, Mahatma Gandhi, Steve Jobs and Richard Branson, to name but a few. The power of story-telling has been harnessed for as long as homo sapiens have been around (you only need to consider wall paintings and oral history). So the new developments in the neurosciences around how our brains mirror some of the activities within stories creating bonds that can lead to changed beliefs, attitudes and behaviors is really no more than a confirmation of what has always been known.

The question is; which guides and stories do you wish to believe?

The current dominant story line goes something like this. The free-market is the only way to secure economic freedom; necessary to enable any other kind of freedom for the individual. Economic growth is therefore paramount. There is no alternative. This is the only route to gain great individual and organizational wealth. So, if you want to be one of 'us' you must buy-in to this view.

This does indeed tap into our need to be an 'us' rather than a 'them', our fears of being at the bottom of the pecking order, our passive greed, and the view that this makes perfect sense (a form of collective self-deception). Remember our discussion on 'imagined realities' in the Introduction, filtered through our 'episodic' memory in section I. So long as the media and others in positions of power offer a consistent message, whilst silencing any other voices, there will be little opportunity for dissonance.

So, if you are one of those who do not buy-in to this dominant view you are considered as either eccentric (in which case you can be ignored) or extreme (in which case you need to be outlawed).

It is important to recognize that this is indeed simply the 'current' dominant story line. Stories change over time depending, predominantly, on the needs and wants of those with the most influence. And it is their stories that become the hegemonic 'truth.' This can be seen as either bad news or good news. Bad news in that those with the most influence can stifle any other ideas and story lines. This in turn can make the 'silent majority' feel powerless to cultivate change. Which in turn can lead to apathy, passivity, denial or culpability in the form of blame (and scapegoating). But good news in that we can view the current story line as transient thereby offering hope, determination and resilience in bringing forth new story lines. Which in turn can lead to a renewal of energy, focus and action through building 'bridges', coalitions and trust.

So are there alternative story-tellers out there with more positive stories to tell?

I wholeheartedly say yes! Yes, there are. You only have to consider;

- Yuval Noah Harari and his historic and evolutionary account of homo sapiens, cultural change and our potential next step as a species.
- Or Colin Wilson who has been side-lined to a great extent for being a great champion of the power of the individual and human potential generically to transform our lives individually and collectively.
- Or Owen Jones, a left-wing columnist and anti-establishment activist, dismissed for his 'ramblings' on the need for a democratic revolution to reclaim those "rights and powers annexed by the Establishment"; a new way of

doing politics.

- Or the Green House Think Tank set up to challenge "the ideas that have created the world we live in now, and offering positive alternatives", including that new economic concept 'de-growth.'

It is interesting that much of our current story as laid out above comes about through a misunderstanding of the Adam Smith dictum 'greed is good', hidden beneath lots of justifications and self-deception. What Adam Smith actually said was more complex than that. On the one hand he said competition would return the price of anything to 'its normal price', and on the other hand that we would act according to 'the dictates of our moral faculties to restrain our selfishness'. A far cry from 'greed is good.' Nevertheless, it is this above all else that has led to our obsession with individualism, self-interest and economic growth. But a growth that has little to do with the quality of the life of much of society.

There are many many more voices that are being silences, but the greatest voice of all we need to start paying more attention to is our own. I truly believe that my story has value and should be heard. That your story has value and should be heard. And that it is unacceptable for 1% of the population to think their story is the only one worth hearing, and that it stands separate to yours and mine. We need to embrace our own stories and their inter-connectedness, oneness, and in terms of team and organizational development, our interdependence with others stories. This shows the true sense of growth and maturity through a commitment to transforming the self to transform the world we live in for the betterment of all of us.

How do we do this in a world where cultures are coalescing into less and less mega-cultures, but splitting off into more and more micro-cultures? Not the mini-cultures of our ancestors which worked to an 'optimal' number of 150 people. Rather these are invented communities and virtual communities, not actual, physical and intimate communities reflecting the networked organizations we can expect for the future. This is a shift from big 'us' and 'them' to lots and lots of 'mini-us' and 'mini-them' where we are bound by global interests, problems and cultures. For this to work we need an equal shift, as noted in section U, in the 'I – It' dynamic to one of 'I – Thou' where we see 'them' as subjects and not objects through the integration of left/right brain thinking. This is sometimes referred to as the 'Will to Consciousness' or the integration of our masculine/ feminine sides, our objective/ subjective minds, the everyday/ and our power consciousness.

It is interesting that the recognition of identity as socially constructed power dynamics is a relatively new phenomenon. And in accepting the male/female masculine/feminine binary early feminists caved in to the construction of a reality based on the dominant group; into the prevailing hegemony. Anthropologists have long accepted that there is no one way of performing femininity, masculinity or hegemonic heterosexuality (challenging western assumptions on gender, such as the Polynesian Mahu and the North American Berdache) rather it is dependent on time and place, i.e. situational. Kimam males are a prime example of heterosexuals engaging in homosexual behavior as part of their masculinization process, while the Hijra are a good example of the confrontation of femaleness and maleness in the same body. These examples challenge the very nature of Western thinking which tries hard to resolve contradictions (left brain thinking), while Hinduism, for example, allows opposites to confront each other without a resolution (creative right brain thinking).

So what we require is a shift from a 'binary and boundary system' to an 'integrated system' that would counteract our in/out either/or psychology much of current Western cultures are based on, so allowing for a conscious act of suspended judgement. This is very much in line with what we know about eusociality (eu is the Greek word for 'good', so 'good society') and eukaryotic cells (which make up our bodies) as explained by Hofstede, Hofstede and Minkov in *Cultures and Organizations*. This takes us out of the field of competition and into collaboration. Very much at odds with how too many of us currently think and behave.

It is recognized in the education sector that whenever Ofsted descend, it is just four weeks too soon. If only...

Nevertheless, Ofsted did appear and we were judged 'good' with some high praise for leadership interventions, safeguarding and aspects of teaching, learning and assessment. As the Inspection Nominee I was pleased and relieved, and knew it was time to move on. I handed in my notice, set up my business, lifted up my 'C' and got down to writing my book.

In less than six months I had secured paying clients, consultancy contracts, fully completed the first draft of my book, and run half a dozen DISC workshops, with the more recent one's focusing on using personality profiling as a tool to support personalized learning targets. Who would have thought it? Yet on reflection is that not what my journey illustrates?

I am now able to tap into my determined, decisive, doer secondary 'D' trait, while feeling an inspired, interested and at all times fun loving 'I', with a steady, stable approach that means I am now able to support others better. I'm not by nature a 'C' so I don't believe in perfection, but I have lifted my conscientious detailed planning trait and put these to great use. DISC has indeed transformed my life, and importantly transformed me to the 'I' I really want to be.

My key learning point:

My circuitous life journey no longer seems a failure but an interesting route map on the road to an even more interesting future.

Transformation can only happen after raised self-awareness, self-acceptance, focused attention and the development of your inner being that allows us to shift from 'I-It' to 'I-Thou' to truly embrace interconnectedness. For only then can we be our own guides for the betterment of us all.

What is your key learning point?

_____

_____

_____

_____

_____

_____

Chapter Twenty-five

Y - Yen Cultures

Lots of educators use the quip, practice makes perfect. However, as I have stated on numerous occasions now practice does not make perfect. Practice makes permanent. This is much better news for those who have a true 'yearning for growth', for growth has never been about perfection but about a process; practice makes permanent and leads to further growth. However, bizarrely a lack of practice does not lead to impermanence. A lack of practice simply leads to a permanent 'default' mode and stagnation.

'Yearning for growth' is an interesting phrase when we consider it against my earlier comment in the last section about the Green House Think Tank's de-growth strategy. In fact Rupert Read, author of *What is 'Growth' for and can we afford it?: A critical twenty first century assessment of the hegemonic economic policy of our time*, actually talks about 'post-growth' in the reports he presented which were "designed to show that an alternative to the false dichotomy between growth and austerity is necessary, possible and desirable." He further goes on to say, "We want to offer people a better life. A life that is based on having fewer material possessions and less formal economic activity, but more well-being, more community, more security, and much more of what Ivan Illich rightly called 'conviviality'." Or what we might think of as more neighbourliness in its widest sense. Indeed, we might think now is a perfect time for a rethink when even The Spectator can comment on the 'new conservative madness' where 'all over the world, conservativism is having a nervous breakdown.'

So de-growth in terms of economic policy, growth in terms of social wealth.

Leadership if we remember, to quote Travis Bradberry, was "a process of social influence which maximizes the efforts of others toward the achievement of a greater good" where leaders became social agents. And culture remember has something to do with cumulative, collective and time-bound behavior that has been learnt through repetition. This reflects the sociologist Pierre Bourdieu's notion of 'symbolic violence' which shapes 'habitus' which is a force exerted on the body directly played out in the 'field' and which generates "a permanent disposition, a durable way of standing, speaking, walking, and thereby of feeling and thinking." This leads to 'extraordinary inertia' (see Bourdieu's *The Logic of Practice*). However, we can break this inertia through reflection and supplementation (a term derived from the philosopher Jacques Derrida) where new knowledge acts on existing knowledge to de-stabilize the old.

It is interesting that this reflects much of the current thinking around inter-cultural understanding and becoming informed global citizens, especially as espoused by the young. An example being AMP Global Youth who are currently running programs to develop young global leaders. Of course youth has its own problems. Indeed, it could be tantamount to treason not to say that youth have become known as 'a problem', and that this problem is to do with the relationship between youth and adults over issues of control and power.

Our current perception of young people is a prime example of binary thinking. We have the good, well-educated and disciplined white middle class heterosexual child, and the bad, poorly educated delinquent, who is invariably black or working class. We discussed the notion of subcultures earlier. Let us now consider the notion of youth subculture. These are invariably heteronormative and class bound. However, queer subcultures on the other hand can be seen to cross class, race, sexuality, gender and generational bounds which allow for a new way to redefine the binary of adolescence and adulthood, through a prolonged period of sub-cultural participation, and enables theorists and participants to move beyond the separation of both youth and adulthood, expert and participant. So in fact not a subculture, or even a sub-subculture, but rather a contra-culture; a conscious antagonism to the wider society, or a creative critique of dominant culture. You only have to consider the difference between Punk (with its ritualistic language of the rejected) and Queer Punk (a critique of both hetero and homo-normativity). That is, a critique not just of the view that heterosexuality is the norm, but also the norms associated with the mainstream assimilated LGBT community, where both stigmatize certain types of self-expression that violate these norms. This is a form of resistance at the individual and collective levels over time to cultivate a slow cross-cultural transformation of societal values. Or the conceptual difference between body manipulation and cosmetic surgery. Or the great strides in mass mobilization and crowd funding platforms.

These offer real insights into the possibilities of cultivating positive change through leaders as social agents, and the need for our leaders to have a strength of character to stand up to the norms; to dare to be different. Embracing our uniqueness then becomes a defining value, when aligned to the value of oneness or interconnectedness. This has little to do with current thinking about individualism and self-obsession (it is worth remembering that during the Classical Age 'man' did not exist as a thinking subject on itself. It wasn't really until the philosopher Emanuel Kant that the modern concept of the 'self' developed, as 'free and to be free is to think for oneself', that is, as an autonomous individual. He would be aghast though at where this has led us). It has everything to do with self-actualisation that takes us beyond a preoccupation with 'me'; enabling us to become social agents through becoming more fully who we are. Or as Joseph Campbell the great American mythologist and writer of *The Hero With a Thousand Faces* put it in 1949;

When we quit thinking primarily about ourselves and our own self-preservation, we undergo a truly heroic transformation of consciousness.

My key learning point:

For an 'I', not thinking about me can be supremely difficult but recognizing, feeling and living this has allowed me to focus on the benefit of the gift to others, rather than on the giving of the gift for me.

Moving beyond the self allows for our initial transformation to become sustainable for the betterment of us all.

What is your key learning point?

_____

_____

_____

_____

_____

_____

Chapter Twenty-six

Z - Zazzy Cultures

Most of us will have heard the Shakespeare phrase 'all that (glitters) is not gold.' How many of us, though, have been distracted by that wonderful 'must have', only to find it's been a masquerade once we have hold of it? This is because we sometimes lose sight of what is important to us 'based on our core values', driven by false needs and false motivations. We need to understand better that these false needs and motivations are encouraged as a means to stop us from reaching full consciousness. For people who have developed, what Paulo Freire calls, critical consciousness become too questioning, problematic and influential. They challenge the status quo. They are not willing to accept the old argument 'there is no alternative.'

Freire suggests there are four levels of consciousness; magical (where we experience ourselves as impotent to do anything about our personal and socio-economic position, where we are controlled by outside forces); naive (where we are able to make a distinction between ourselves and the outside world. We believe some things are within our reach, that we can do something about parts of our situation, but are convinced there are lot of other things we are not capable of doing or having); critical (where we realize we are able to change things, have a growing understanding of our own capabilities and potential, recognize our oppression, what role we have played in this, and how we can now fight against this with positive and productive action); and political consciousness (where we discover other shared realities and shared problems. This leads to people combining their strengths to influence change for the betterment of us all). According to Freire,

"Nobody liberates nobody, nobody liberates themselves alone: human beings liberate themselves in communion."

This is a salutary lesson for all of us who think we have 'progressed, developed or grown' in consciousness. For without the sustainability of reflective practices based on a true sense of integrity and honesty we are likely to 'slip.' The purpose here is not to criticize, but to remind us of the need for self-compassion and positive action in lifting ourselves up again and getting back on our life-long journey towards being more truly ourselves, who we truly have the potential to be, our uniqueness that is a healthy tension of difference and sameness that allows us to fully interconnect with a sense of neighborliness that is based on the good of all. This is the true meaning of freedom for me. Free to choose to take positive action for the betterment of us all.

This sets out clearly my idealistic values. It is important though to continually revisit these to ensure my beliefs and behavior (operational values) reflect them.

Idealistic values	Operational beliefs and behavior
Personal Growth	Am I continually learning and developing? And challenging myself into my stretch zone in a way that shifts learning into action?
Integrity	Do I truly reflect on my thoughts and actions with a level of self-detachment to ensure they are directed at better meeting the needs of all in given situations? And do my actions convey this, or merely serve my own needs?
Honesty	Am I brutally honest in a fashion that quashes growth, or truly honest in a way that cultivates positive action in myself and others?

Compassion	Do my thoughts, words and actions show compassion, or do I have internal talk that looks to put others or myself down, to blame and to criticize?
Positivity	Are my thoughts and actions really positive ones, or do I fall into limiting beliefs? I will need to continually review my thoughts and actions with integrity.
To be more truly me; unique	This requires true acceptance, repetitive self-reflection and sound self-awareness. Am I really daring to be different? Am I really savoring my sameness?
Interconnectedness	How do my actions impact on others, and who do I connect with? Or am I still thinking in terms of 'us and them' and 'I and it'?
Neighborliness	Are my actions really based on the good of us all, or justifications based on my own self-deception?
Freedom	This will require continued reminder of what constitutes freedom and what I am willing to do and give up to attain an appropriate measure if it. The choices I make.
Sustainability	Am I doing all the above in a manner that reenergizes and rejuvenates my endeavors and my life and the lives of others in a way that supports the betterment of life for us all?

Self-reflection

To better elicit your own idealistic and operational values you might want to consider the following questions:

Idealistic values – consider something specific, i.e. your ideal business goal, your ideal career...

- What is most important to you about this...?
- How does that make you feel?
- What do you get out of it?
- What else?
- If you were able to do..., that would give you a sense of... What?

Operational values – consider something specific in your day to day life, i.e. your job...

- What makes you (go into work) day after day?
- What do you get out of it?
- What else?
- What do you like/ dislike about...?
- What would have to happen to make you (leave your job)?

It is paramount we all strive for higher, critical, political, power or super consciousness (or whichever term best suits you) in order to make sense of our own personality, history, failings, dysfunctions and purpose, and to challenge the accepted 'facts' and 'truths' we live our lives by. For how else can we progress? How else can we resist the currently prevailing and negative interests of the dominant group in society? For how else can we knock the status quo and equilibrium off course, to 'cultivate positive and productive culture/s' which are of benefit to us all?

My key learning point:

It is important for me to turn the writings in this book into actionable steps as a way to ensure I do not 'slip' back or lose focus, which would be too easy for a default 'I', to sustain progressive, positive and purposeful action.

We need to redefine both our idealistic values and operational actions to focus on doing the right thing.

What is your key learning point?

_____

_____

_____

_____

_____

_____

Part Three

Pulling it all together

This book has primarily been about the kind of person 'I' want to be and we want to be, and the kind of leaders we need for a better future whether that be in life in general, in business and in organizations, or indeed in politics or any other field, and therefore the kind of cultures we want to cultivate for the betterment of us all.

One of the key questions asked was how an understanding of the self through DISC can help bring this about. I see personality profiling as the starting point as this opens up a space to see our default settings (our basic wiring as it were) and thereby DISCover who we really are. Acceptance of our default settings is fundamental before any change can occur. Just as knowing and learning from our own journey will be enhanced through gaining a deep understanding of why our past may have mapped out as it did, and can therefore act as a guide for our present and future choices. As I mentioned earlier my story is of importance, your story is of importance and the interconnectedness of all our stories is at the heart of cultivating the positive and productive cultures we deserve and desire.

The key learning points from my journey that have created my story and led to my A to Z Framework and its sub-models were:

A We need to know our 'default' approach from which to adapt to suit current and changing needs.

B We need to expand our field of comfort through stretch and challenge or our comfort zone soon becomes our prison zone.

C We need to embrace complexity if we want to survive and thrive.

D We need to stop tolerating and start embracing diversity to truly capitalize on its and our potential.

E   We need to accept our fixed mindset to expand our growth mindset.

F   We need to eliminate blame from our thinking in order to enhance our capacity for trust.

G   We need to develop our self-reflective practices to be able to grow.

H   We need to clarify our true 'why' so enabling the buy-in of others.

I   We need stories to give meaning to our lives, to affirm our identities, and to validate our values and purpose.

J   We need to be the new wise men and women who shape our future stories in order to cultivate the positive and productive cultures we deserve.

K   We need to recognize that it is our true personality traits that are our greatest assets. These need to be nurtured and developed.

L   We need to know ourselves before we can hope to actively and purposefully adapt to our environment.

M   We need to better understand and integrate our bodies senses into our decision-making processes.

N   We need to take a leap of faith to become our own future story-telling wise ones.

O   We need to cultivate a sense of responsibility, ownership and belief that allows for a transformational leap.

P   We need to pay attention to what 'truly' motivates ourselves and others. This is the most effective way to secure real success.

Q   We need to embrace the spirit of synthesis, where the whole is greater than the sum of the parts.

R   We need to reframe our emotional and thinking and behavioral responses before we can feel, think or act differently.

S   We need to embrace the paradox of change.

T   We need to identify and 'name' our sub-personalities so

we can then dis-identify with them.

U We need to challenge our own thinking and justification processes.

V We already have our own answers embedded in our own stories.

W Knowing our purpose is insufficient, we must live our purpose. That is the true win-win.

X Transformation can only happen after raised self-awareness, self-acceptance, focused attention and the development of your inner being that allows us to shift from 'I-It' to 'I-Thou' to truly embrace interconnectedness. For only then can we be our own guides for the betterment of us all.

Y Moving beyond the self allows for our initial transformation to become sustainable for the betterment of us all.

Z We need to redefine both our inspirational values and operational actions to focus on doing the right thing.

The problems to be solved, as I see them, in order to be able to cultivating those positive and productive cultures are:

Stage 1 - Knowing yourself and self-mastery.
Stage 2 - Knowing your why and how to influence others.
Stage 3 - Knowing your sticking points and moving on.
Stage 4 - Knowing your energy flow and sustaining success.

The A to Z Framework offers a stepping stone approach to addressing and solving these problems, with DISC personality profiling as the starting point.

Self-reflection

What are your key learning points?
And how do they combine to form your story?

Stage 1

• Knowing yourself and self-mastery.

DISC personality profiling allows for a starting point from which to self-reflect. There are many and varied tools and strategies for raising self-awareness and self-knowledge from which we can develop self-mastery. This allows us to have more control over our choices and in our lives. Control over our choices and lives drives up our sense of self-worth, self-belief and the freedom we perceive to exist in shaping our lives, as an individual and as a leader. As you will know, with great freedom comes great responsibility and self-mastery enables you to accept, embrace and fully live your choices.

Stage 2

• Knowing your why and how to influence others.

There is little point having control over our choices if we have no purpose in which to direct these choices. Developing a deeper understanding of our values and beliefs will help shape an understanding of your purpose (your why). When you begin to align your aspirational values and your operational values your thinking and behavior will take on more meaningful, purposeful and influential characteristics that will better connect to other people's desire for meaning. You will become a force to be heard, having greater impact as a consequence.

Stage 3

• Knowing your sticking points and moving on.

The **MIRROR Model** is an extended model that delves deeper into Stages 1 and 2, before elaborating through mastery, intervention, reframing, repetition and opportunity to reenergize. Self-mastery, as noted above, allows for more control over our choices. When we align this to knowing our purpose we have a strengthened driver for interventions. Nevertheless, as with all changes and new roads there is likely to be 'slippage' and 'sticking points.' Reframing at these times will support sustained progress that will enable repetition of actions and interventions that will lead to new opportunities. This is a spiraling model that takes you further and further out of your comfort zone, building mastery of the self and the model itself to enable growth and expanded success of your purpose.

Stage 4

- Knowing your energy flow and sustaining success.

Part and parcel of the MIRROR spiraling model is a greater understanding of the interconnection between our body, mind and spirit to reenergize and reconnect our energy flow. This is a great transformational stage that will connect you to me, us to them and I to Thou, engaging in the interconnectedness of all people and all things. This stage more than any other will truly allow us to see the kind of cultures we want to cultivate for the betterment of us all.

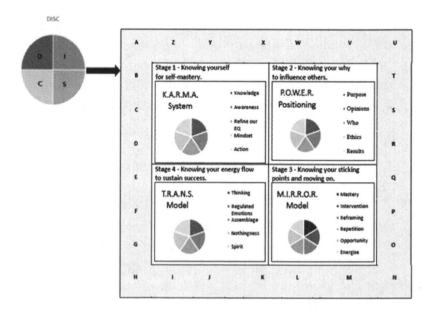

Parting Comments

In his book *The Personality Code* Travis Bradberry laments never having met Dr. William Marston, the creator of DISC, Wonder Woman and the Lie Detector but offers us a great story of Dorothy whose life was impacted greatly by meeting Dr. Marston in hospital during his final days. The impact we can have on one another, whether that is up close or at a distance was echoed, not by Dorothy, but by Glinda and Elphaba, in the great show 'Wicked' when they sing 'For Good.'

As I mentioned earlier change is often forced upon us but growth is a choice. I have been supremely lucky in my life to have had many learning opportunities from which to grow, not least coming upon DISC and the great work that is being done through The Coaching Academy, which has inspired in me a desire to be a better version of me. An 'I' I can be proud of through bringing a healthy tension to the personality I so mismanaged for too many years.

Self-awareness, self-development and self-mastery only have relevance within the interplay with others, and self-transformation in any spiritual sense, as Roberto Assagioli noted, needs a practical application for it to be of worth. At the start of this book I said it was my responsibility, your responsibility as leaders and our responsibility collectively to transform ourselves to transform our businesses and organizations to transform the world we live in for the better. Having worked my way through this book, lifting up my C greatly in doing so, I believe this even more so now. The acceptance of a status quo that is not meeting the needs of the vast majority of people on this planet is reprehensible at any time, but more so once you have raised yourself out of the states of 'cognitive and emotional miser.'

Let us all strive for the positive and productive culture/s we truly desire and deserve.

From the Author: Thank you for purchasing 'DISCover the Power of You'. My sincere hope is that you derived as much from reading this book as I have in creating it. If you have a few moments, please feel free to add your review of the book at your favorite online site for feedback. Also, if you would like to connect with other books that I have coming in the near future, please visit my website for news on upcoming works, recent blog posts and to sign up for my free eBook: http://www.robertadams.uk.com

Sincerely, Robert Adams

Suggested Reading List

Bev James (2011) *DO IT! OR DITCH IT*, Virgin Books
This is a brilliant book for anyone interested in setting up or running a business, indeed for anyone intent on achieving success in any area of their life through a greater understanding of their own personality traits.

Charles Handy (1999) *Understanding Organizations* 4th Edition, Penguin Books
Although times change and my hope is that the future of organizations will be dramatically different from many of those discussed in this hugely influential book, this is still a must for anyone wishing to understand organizations, organizational cultures and development.

Colin Wilson (2015) *Super Consciousness; The Quest for the Peak Experience*, Watkins
An amazing writer and book for anyone interested in a truly positive slant on human potential.

Daniel Goleman (1995) *Emotional Intelligence*, Bloomsbury
This book changed the way we looked at intelligence and allowed for a much greater understanding and positive portrayal of emotions in decision making.

Jeffrey Sugerman, Mark Scullard and Emma Wilhelm (2011) *The 8 Dimensions of Leadership*, Berrett-Koehler Publishers, Inc
A great book for any leader who has a drive to learn more about their own personality and behavior, and the behavior of others to become more effective.

John Whitmore (2009) *Coaching for Performance*, Nicholas Brealey

Publishing

The seminal book on coaching to improve performance and transform leadership.

Particia Bossons, Patricia Riddell and Denis Sartain (2015) *The Neuroscience of Leadership Coaching*, Bloomsbury Publishing

A fascinating read for those interested in getting the best out of people through coaching aligned to new research on how the brain works.

Stephen R. Covey (1997) *The 7 Habits of Highly Effective People*, Franklin Covey

This is a highly insightful book full of wisdom, with that practical element that truly makes this book useful.

Tara Swart, Kitty Chisholm and Paul Brown (2015) *Neuroscience for Leadership*, Palgrave MacMillan

This is a must-read for all leaders with any interest in knowing and harnessing how the brain works to support decision-making, culture-making and success.

Travis Bradberry's (2007) *The Personality Code*, Putnam and (2009) Emotional Intelligence 2, TalentSmart

These books are an absolute must for anyone interested in raising their self-awareness, unlocking the secrets of people reading and making use of these to improve performance and ensure success.

Yuval Noah Harari (2011) *Sapiens: A Brief History of Humankind*, Vintage Books

Story-telling at its best. A must read for anyone intent on creating a better future.

**BUSINESS
BOOKS**

15 Ways to Own Your Future
Take Control of Your Destiny in Business and in Life
Michael Khouri
A 15-point blueprint for creating better collaboration,
enjoyment, and success in business and in life.
Paperback: 978-1-78535-300-0 ebook: 978-1-78535-301-7

Common Excuses of the Comfortable Compromiser
The Understanding Why People Oppose Your Great Idea
Matt Crossman
Comfortable compromisers block the way of anyone trying to
change anything. This is your guide to their common excuses.
Paperback: 978-1-78099-595-3 ebook: 978-1-78099-596-0

The Failing Logic of Money
Duane Mullin
Money is wasteful and cruel, causes war, crime and
dysfunctional feudalism. Humankind needs happiness, peace
and abundance. So banish money and use technology and
knowledge to rid the world of war, crime and poverty.
Paperback: 978-1-84694-259-4 ebook: 978-1-84694-888-6

Mastering the Mommy Track
Juggling Career and Kids in Uncertain Times
Erin Flynn Jay
Mastering the Mommy Track tells the stories of everyday working
mothers, the challenges they have faced, and lessons learned.
Paperback: 978-1-78099-123-8 ebook: 978-1-78099-124-5

Modern Day Selling
Unlocking Your Hidden Potential
Brian Barfield
Learn how to reconnect sales associates with customers and
unlock hidden sales potential.
Paperback: 978-1-78099-457-4 ebook: 978-1-78099-458-1

**The Most Creative, Escape the Ordinary, Excel at Public
Speaking Book Ever**
All The Help You Will Ever Need in Giving a Speech
Philip Theibert
The 'everything you need to give an outstanding speech' book,
complete with original material written by a professional
speechwriter.
Paperback: 978-1-78099-672-1 ebook: 978-1-78099-673-8

On Business And For Pleasure
A Self-Study Workbook for Advanced Business English
Michael Berman
This workbook includes enjoyable challenges and has been
designed to help students with the English they need for work.
Paperback: 978-1-84694-304-1

Small Change
Big Deal Money as if People Mattered
Jennifer Kavanagh
Money is about relationships: between individuals and between communities. Small is still beautiful, as peer lending model, microcredit, shows.
Paperback: 978-1-78099-313-3 ebook: 978-1-78099-314-0